THY ROD
AND THY CREEL

Other books by Odell Shepard:

A LONELY FLUTE (verse)
SHAKESPEARE QUESTIONS
BLISS CARMAN
THE HARVEST OF A QUIET EYE
THE JOYS OF FORGETTING
THE LORE OF THE UNICORN

THY ROD
AND THY CREEL

ODELL SHEPARD

Nick Lyons Books
Winchester Press

First published 1930 by Edwin Valentine Mitchell, Inc.
Introduction copyright © 1984 by Paul Schullery

ALL RIGHTS RESERVED. No part of this book may be used or reproduced in any manner whatsoever without prior written permission from the publisher except in the case of brief quotations embodied in critical reviews and articles. All inquiries should be addressed to New Century Publishers, Inc., 220 Old New Brunswick Road, Piscataway, New Jersey 08854.

Produced by
Nick Lyons Books
31 W. 21st Street
New York, NY 10011

Published and distributed by
Winchester Press
New Century Publishers, Inc.
220 Old New Brunswick Road
Piscataway, NJ 08854

Printed In The United States Of America
10 9 8 7 6 5 4 3 2 1

LC#: 84-60996

To Leslie Badmington and David Keeney,
TWO GOOD FRIENDS AND GOOD FISHERMEN,
LOYAL AND DEVOTED SONS OF CONNECTICUT,
I DEDICATE THIS BOOK ABOUT A SPORT
THEY LOVE

"Some fishing is better than others, but there is no such thing as bad fishing."
—FRANCIS FRANCIS

Introduction

by Paul Schullery

In the world of angling literature the republication of Odell Shepard's *Thy Rod and Thy Creel,* first published in 1930, is a major event. The book's story is a quiet one. It was written in a quiet spirit, a spirit that seems a direct response to Walton's admonition to "study to be quiet" (though Walton did not mean "study to be silent," for he was not silent himself). It was published quietly. And it slipped, very quietly, into oblivion. It is even possible that it will have a quiet career this second time around, for its author and his book were set aside from the general clamor of popular writing in his tone and direction. The world of angling literature, as he knew, is considerably smaller than the world of fishing writing.

Yet having it back is still a major event, because it is such an extraordinary book that its mere presence—however widely or narrowly it may be read—enriches the sport and provides at least the potential for the elevation of angling thought above its customary levels.

Those who have heard of Shepard's book probably did so because of Arnold Gingrich. In *The Fishing in Print* he praised it lavishly:

> Today I can think of nobody who has written about angling more beautifully than Odell Shepard, at least since Walton, and I have almost the same feeling about Shepard's book that I have about Walton's, that it is almost a disservice to quote from it, because like the *Compleat Angler* itself, it should be swallowed whole, and then savored again at leisure.

I will not succumb to the temptation, as Arnold did, of quoting Shepard. Indeed I don't have to, because here at last is the whole book, to be savored, swallowed, and (to pursue Arnold's culinary metaphor) digested at will.

As Arnold admitted, he only came to know of *Thy Rod and Thy*

Creel through William Humphrey, a prominent American novelist who occasionally writes angling literature himself (*The Spawning Run; My Moby Dick*). I must admit that even after I had read Arnold's glowing praise of the book I still didn't read it until Bill recommended it to me, too. I was among the fortunate few, then, with access to a copy, but now we are all fortunate, for it can be easily obtained, probably more easily than when it was first published.

Arnold (I never met him, but I have trouble calling him "Gingrich") suggested that it may have been the book's title that doomed it. *Thy Rod and Thy Creel* sounds more than faintly ecclesiastical, so that one is inclined to suspect that even if it is about fishing it must be burdened with religious lessons, which means that it isn't really about fishing at all. I think Arnold could also have suggested that Shepard was not part of the fishing-writing *literati* of his day and so did not see the book serialized or touted by the right people. It may also have been that the publisher made no effort to sell the book. Or it could just have been that the author did not particularly care how the book sold; it was not a part of his "important" work as a writer, and was not even topically similar to the rest of his work. It was after all just a personal statement he wanted to make about fishing.

Shepard was busy succeeding at things other than fishing writing. He was born in farm country near Rock Falls, Illinois, on July 22, 1884, and graduated with various degrees from Northwestern University, the University of Chicago, and Harvard (he later added a few honorary degrees to these). He worked as an editor and reporter for several midwestern newspapers in the first years of the century, then turned to teaching. Between 1908 and 1925 he taught English at U.S.C., Harvard, Radcliffe, Trinity College, Columbia, and one or two others. In later years he was a Guggenheim Fellow and a Huntington Library Research Fellow. The breadth of his studies and interests is revealed partly in this: he was Lieutenant Governor of Connecticut (1940–1941), an honorary member of the Mohegan tribe, and active in the Civil Liberties

Union. It is revealed more fully in a list of his books: *Shakespeare Questions—An Outline for the Study of Leading Plays; A Lonely Flute* (this was poetry); *Bliss Carman, a Study of His Poetry; The Harvest of a Quiet Eye* (again the quiet spirit); *The Joys of Forgetting; The Lore of the Unicorn* (which is really a book, and a very good one, about unicorns); *Thy Rod and Thy Creel; Pedlar's Progress, the Life of Bronson Alcott* (which won a Pulitzer Prize for biography), *Connecticut Past and Present,* and two books written with his son Willard Shepard, *Holdfast Gaines* and *Jenkins Ear.* He edited numerous collections of prose and poetry as well. He died on July 19, 1967.

Thy Rod and Thy Creel, though now compared to Walton's book in quality, is little like Walton's book in anything else. It is a series of meditations on fishing, not instruction in how to use tackle. Shepard explores why fishing is attractive (he defines fishing, for the purpose of this book, as trout fishing) and what kind of person it attracts. Shepard was not overly concerned with quantification, especially in any statistical sense, of who fishermen are. He was more concerned with what fishing's possibilities are, and who is inclined to search for them. He was rarely argumentative, though often profoundly analytical, and never quarrelsome. He succeeded in writing a book that is read for philosophical stimulation as much as for the sheer pleasure of the words.

Ultimately, all that those who love this book say about it must fall short of doing justice to it, and introductions and recommendations and testimonials leave their authors vulnerable to complaint from readers who, when they finally read the book, may exclaim that the half was not told them. As well, I don't suppose that all readers, even all of the most literate readers, will love the book; we are, after all, fishermen, and we take a certain pride in independent thinking. But whether it receives unanimous acceptance or not, *Thy Rod and Thy Creel* is to be welcomed back, not only for its power and eloquence but for its undeniable stature as art. As Arnold said, "If ever there was a book of our century that I'd like to see commended to the anglers of the next, this would have to be it." *Thy Rod and Thy Creel* is that good, for those who seek its special kind of goodness. If you seek intellectual sophistication without social posturing, and wit without sarcasm, and penetrating wisdom without obtuse pedantry, Shepard is your man. If you seek a book that brings life not only to the complexity but to the fun of fishing for trout, *Thy Rod and Thy Creel* is your book.

Livingston, Montana
May, 1984

A TRIAL CAST

ANY man who dares in these days to add yet another book to the literature of angling is likely to give the impression that he is equipped either with an extraordinary knowledge of the sport, such as only a lifetime by the stream-side can now give, or else with an equally phenomenal ignorance of what has been written before him. Half a century ago it was estimated that there must be already at least five hundred books in English about fly-fishing alone, and the intervening decades have probably added half as many more. Since the time of "Dame Juliana Berners," whose classic *Treatyse of Fysshynge wyth an Angle* is now nearing its fifth centenary, every phase of the sport has been thoroughly canvassed and every controversy has been brought to a conclusion or to a draw. Writing a book in this twentieth century about the ancient art of the fisherman is therefore a little like fishing in a widely advertised and popular stream in which all the elder trout are sophisticated and misanthropic creatures, sceptical of everything that looks like a fly.

No angler needs to be told, however, that precisely such shy waters as these often yield the best sport, just because they are difficult and exacting. Always there will be at least one good trout left in them. Always and forever, too, there will be room in the world, and space enough between the fly-books, for one more essay in praise of fishing, even though written by one whose chief equipment is a deep affection for his topic and who has neither the exhaustive knowledge nor the utter ignorance I have mentioned. Good fishermen are likely to be good readers, and they exercise the patience learned elsewhere on behalf of almost any writer who speaks fondly of their sport. They are indulgent toward one who has this taproot of the matter in him, however numerous may be the errors of his which they could easily correct. The best of them do not insist that their author tell them how to catch fish, for they know about that already. They remember that the best book about fishing ever written is hardly to be used as a practical manual—and they may even recall Father Izaak's own words: "Now for the art of catching fish, that is, how to make a man that was none to be an angler by a book, he that undertakes it shall undertake a harder task than Mr. Hales, that in a printed book called *The Private School of Defence* undertook to teach the art of fencing, and was laughed at for his labour. Not but that many useful things might be observed out of that book, but that the art was not to be taught by words; nor is the art of angling."

A TRIAL CAST

What Izaak Walton could not do I shall not attempt. I shall be content to write the rambling, idle, quite unpractical sort of book about fishing that I myself like to read by the fire in winter when the brooks are sealed, or by the stream on drowsy noons—winding into and through the inexhaustible lore of angling as a lazy brook goes through a meadow where the grass is heavy and the reeds are high, pausing and deepening here and there but soon running free again with a glitter of sun on the stickle. There can never be too many books of that good, honest, and leisurely kind.

The meadow brook flows where it must, yet in every rod and yard and foot of its progress it looks, and no doubt feels, free. So do I. The one definite purpose I have in mind as I write these preliminary words is that I will not allow my pen to stray in later pages into a discussion of bait-using, down-stream fishing, or use of the sunken fly. In this one negative respect, at least, my book will be unusual: I shall not defend any of these alleged crimes and misdemeanors. It is enough for me to practise them when occasion demands or serves, as I think most anglers do.—Otherwise, I shall let my flies go where they will, searching every eddy and pocket into which they chance to drift.

There is of course no "public demand" for such a book as I am shadowing forth—but then, all fishermen know what the public is, else they would not show such eagerness to get away from it. Speaking among friends, the general public does not know how to demand any good thing; it does not really want good things until they are provided; and if all writers had paid strict attention to the law of supply and demand we should now have exactly no literature whatever. Consider, furthermore, that there is no great public demand for brook trout, and that what demand there is might be supplied by hatcheries at a huge saving in effort and expense. This book, like fishing itself, is either a luxury or else it is nothing.

Yet I should not like to give the impression that I am what crabbed old Richard Franck, in his famous attack upon Walton, calls "a scribbling putationer . . . deficient in Practicks, and indigent in the lineal and plain Tracts of Experience." The fact is that I am rather rich in such "lineal and plain Tracts," and that I could easily fill all the pages before me with reminiscences of how I took, or lost, this trout and that. Neither should I like to have it thought that I am one who "lays the stress of his arguments upon other men's observations, wherewith he stuffs his indigested octavo and so brings himself under the angler's censure and the common calamity of a plagiary—to be pitied, poor man, for his loss of time in scribbling and transcribing other men's notions." These are hard words, which I hope I shall not deserve any more

A TRIAL CAST

than Izaak Walton did, but they shall not frighten me from digressing at will into other men's notions when I think those notions at least as good as any that I might provide.

A few brothers of the angle who see this book may take it a little hard that I seem to speak of fishing for trout as though there were no other kind of fishing. My title should have indicated to them that I have not tried to cover the whole range of angling in all its kinds, for one does not put a tarpon or a swordfish into a creel, and even the larger salmon and bass are seldom so disposed. Angling, like any other thing, is best defined in its purest and finest examples. Therefore I write chiefly about angling for trout—by which I shall mean, usually, the speckled brook trout of New England and a few other favored regions, known to the learned as *salvelinus fontinalis* and to the pedantic as the "char."

So then, all these things being understood, or at least admitted, I proceed to lengthen my line over this old pool that has been drawn into silver arrows by so many good anglers before me. A fish or two worth taking must still be lurking here.

THREAD OF THE RIVER

I

ONE evening a good many years ago I happened to be rambling in the long English twilight up the banks of the Itchen, most famous of all trout streams. Half a mile or so above the city of Winchester—her bells were clamoring in the afterglow behind me—I saw an angler step down to the river fifty feet before me, rod in hand. Every attitude and motion suggested that he knew what he was about. I stood still to watch him, as an American enthusiast ought to do when he has a chance to see a good English fisherman in action.

His manœuvres were strange to me, accustomed as I then was chiefly to the swift mountain streams of California, where one fishes down-stream perforce, and often with the salmon-roe or a sunken fly. For the first time, I saw a man "fishing the rise" instead of "fishing the water." With extremely fine tackle—his leader glistened like wet gossamer when it looped against the sky—and with casting of the most delicate precision, he dropped his flies here and there on the shining surface, not at random but wherever circled water betrayed the presence of a feeding fish.

Farther and farther up the stream his line reached

out, like an enormously long and nimble finger pointing to the exact spot where a trout had just risen, until he was throwing his flies fully seventy feet through the quiet evening air. Thus he stood and cast for ten minutes, but, although the fish were rising all about, no strike rewarded him. At length I saw him bend and look along the surface of the water to see what flies were "on" or "up," after which he took out his fly-book and sat down to consider. In a few minutes he had chosen a new lure and was casting again, not continuously but at intervals, aiming every cast and allowing his flies to float without drawing. The second flies were no more successful than the first, and again he stooped to look along the surface. This happened several times until, with his fourth or fifth choice of lures, he began to get results. Then I saw him hook and play and net three trout in quick succession, any one of which would have been a prize on almost any American stream, for all of them must have weighed well over a pound. This English angler unhooked them very carefully however, without touching them with his hands, and returned them unharmed to the water. When the last had been brought to net and released he took down his rod and strode off toward home. He had solved the secret of the stream for that evening.

I suppose that one may be instantaneously converted to trout fishing, as one certainly may to love

THREAD OF THE RIVER

or religion, at a time when he thinks he already knows a good deal about it. Before I wandered out that evening along the Itchen I had fished a good many miles of trout-water; I knew my Walton almost by heart and had a fair acquaintance with other piscatorial classics early and late; but while I stood and watched this expert angler it was suddenly borne in upon me that here was a mystery of which I knew almost nothing whatever, that here was a sport carried to the verge of art and well beyond the boundaries of scholarship. I saw that trout-fishing might amount to a good deal more than merely "catching a mess of fish." It had a code, a technique, a tradition, a history. To succeed at it evidently required a good deal more than strong tackle and long patience. Here was scope for intelligence, study, and skill that grows with the years.

What most affected me in this little experience was the charm of its setting. As angling memories usually do, the scene comes back to me now most vividly—the slender river running brimful and lustrous through the afterglow, Saint Catherine's Hill, where the Celtic earthworks are and where John Keats used to walk, glooming down over the water-meadows, the old city near at hand all dimmed by colored mist and hearth-smoke, the rooks rowing home to the elms with rust in their oar-locks, and the tower of the Cathedral scowling down the shallow valley toward St. Cross.

THY ROD AND THY CREEL

What has all this to do with my sudden conversion to angling? Somehow, a good deal—and I think that most fishermen, if they could disentangle the lines and leaders of their recollections, would discover that they owe rather more of their affection for the sport to scenes and environments such as this than they do to heavy baskets.

However this may be with others, I shall never again go fishing or think connectedly about the sport without recalling that scene and the man who taught me, without being aware of my presence, what fishing may be. Neither shall I forget how I walked back through the maze of water-carries into the town and there found the doors of the Cathedral still open, so that I could go at once to the little worn slab in the pavement which records that there lies the body of Izaak Walton, and could see the colored window faintly shining over it, testifying to the affection of his sons who fish in the streams of all the world. Winchester, Walton's grave, and an expert angler using all his art on a June evening beside the Itchen! Leigh Hunt himself, if he had ever encountered such a cluster of associations, might well have recanted his heresies and become a fisherman.

Angling for trout in the chalk streams of South England is such a revelation to the American who sees it for the first time not merely because it is a more highly developed and more difficult sport than he is likely to have known at home. Its charm is partly due to the water itself which, in spite of its gray color, is strangely lustrous in all reflected lights of night and day, and is braided everywhere with trailing waterweeds. Like most of the small rivers that flow from the South Downs, Test and Itchen run exactly full to the brim throughout the year, so that the trout swim within a foot or two of the floor-level of many a low-built house along the banks. Fishing in these streams is entirely different in atmosphere and effect, therefore, from anything to be experienced in the wild western rivers of America, or, for that matter, in the swift waters of Scotland and Devonshire. It is, so to speak, more domestic; at any rate, more civilized. The angler's landmarks in this old rich country are church spires a thousand years of age, which he seldom loses sight of; and if he has the good fortune to live beside the stream he can have better fishing from his own door-step than the American usually finds within five hundred miles.

This reduces the element of adventure almost to zero, to be sure, and makes even the best of English angling tame indeed in comparison with the sport as seen in California, where it is combined necessarily with hardy mountaineering. And yet this very tameness has a charm. To take the wildest and wariest of fish from a stream that has been turning grist-mills since Roman days, from water up which the Vikings poled their war-boats a thousand years ago, from a split and parcelled and man-handled little stream—this is a surprise and a perennially delightful one. It reminds me of an experience I had once at Concord, Massachusetts, one of the oldest and best of American towns. I was sitting on the piazza of the Colonial Inn there, talking to a friend about a fishing trip we were planning into the wilds of Canada, and while we were talking the proprietor of the inn came up the walk carrying a cheap wooden pole under one arm and a newspaper parcel under the other. We assumed that he had been plugging for horn-pout in one of the adjacent ponds, or perhaps dapping for pickerel in the river, and asked him what he had caught. Spreading out the newspaper, he revealed a brook trout in perfect condition and weighing a little over one pound, together with three other trout of eight or nine inches. Where had he caught these? "Oh, over in the mill-dam." Every morning, he said, it was his custom to go and sit by the mill-dam brook to read his newspaper, and he always took his pole along, baited his hook with worms, and let nature take her course. Very seldom did he return without at least one good trout, and some days he had half a dozen.—Well, this mill-dam brook is about three feet across in the wider places; it flows down through a dozen or more back yards, including one that once belonged to Ralph Waldo Emerson, in its course from the woods to the

THREAD OF THE RIVER

river; the shops and pavement of Concord's main street are built over it; for a longer time than almost any other American stream it has been accessible to the angler and to the small boy and the house cat; so far as I know, it has never been stocked. Was Henry Thoreau aware that it contained good trout? If he was, he never said so, even in his private journal.

The quietness and domesticity of trout-fishing in England is important to American anglers because there can be no doubt that the traditions of the sport were developed in that country, most of the implements and methods were devised there, and most of the classic literature of angling has been written by Englishmen. It is true that the technique, and still more what may be called the ceremonial, of fishing had been carried far in France before England began to fish for pleasure; but this is what we may say of several other sports. The Frenchman has always been a stickler for convention, form, and routine in his outdoor diversions, which seem to have for him primarily an æsthetic value, whereas the Englishman goes in rather more for tangible results. This difference is illustrated by the tale of the Englishman who was invited by his French host to take a turn with the gun over his country estate and shoot hares. One hundred yards from the house a well-grown hare came bounding across the path, and up went the visitor's gun; but the host cried out to him excitedly: "Don't shoot!

Don't shoot! That's Mimi. We never shoot at Mimi." A few minutes later another hare was sighted, and again the blood-thirsty Englishman was about to pull the trigger, but again he was admonished in tones of shocked reprobation: "No, no, no! That's Clarice. We never shoot at Clarice." Deciding that he had found his way into a menagerie where all the animals were strictly preserved, the visitor made no effort to bag the next hare that presented itself, and he was amazed to hear the host shouting to him over the bang-bang of a dozen guns: "Oh, shoot! Shoot! That's Alphonse. We *always* shoot at Alphonse."

Although not of English origin—or, for that matter, of French, if we go back far enough—the sport of angling has taken on a decidedly English character during the last four or five hundred years, and it seems today, wherever we find it at its best, an expression of the English temper—placid, meditative, somewhat learned, slightly whimsical, governed by an unwritten code of honor, informed entirely by the amateur spirit, offering endless opportunity for the camouflage of sensibility and refinement under the disguise of a manly sport. It comes to us from a land where men ride their hobby-horses very hard, where they turn scholarship into play and play into scholarship. The really devoted and passionate angler, though he may fish in New Zealand or California, in New Brunswick or the Swiss Lakes or Iceland, is almost al-

THREAD OF THE RIVER

ways a person who works harder at his play than he does, or than other men do, at business. This is to say that he is a hobby-rider, and that again is a way of saying that he is either English by birth and training or else he has succumbed, quite possibly without knowing it, to an English influence.

Where but in England could there have been conducted such a contest as that held some fifty years ago on the Lea, Izaak Walton's stream? Two hundred and seventy-six anglers, each of whom had paid a large entrance fee, were stationed thirty feet apart along either bank and fished for roach there from dawn to sunset, the prize of forty pounds being awarded to a contestant who had taken thirteen ounces of fish. Where else in the world is such extreme care and learning lavished upon the exact imitation of natural flies—much of it wasted, no doubt, according to American opinion—or to the minute details of equipment? The fact is that thousands of Englishmen feel about fishing very much as others do about music and poetry and painting, and that they give to it much the same unstinting devotion as that shown toward the supreme arts. When we consider that not only the born sportsman does this, but men of the highest eminence in serious pursuits—any one can name Lord Grey of Falloden, Andrew Lang, and Charles Kingsley among the anglers of this sort without going back more than sixty years—it becomes a question, at least in the

THY ROD AND THY CREEL

minds of those who are not themselves initiated, what sort of fascination there can be in this sport that has won and held such devotion.

II

THE charm of angling, and the strong hold it takes upon many of us, have never been exactly explained. This is not because angling is mysterious in its nature, like poetry, but because its fascination is so inclusive, woven of so many strands. We attribute the pleasure it gives us to one cause after another, but after each attempt at an explanation we are obliged to say: "Well no; it is not entirely that. There is something more."

I have heard men attempt to account for fishing by reference to our supposed "ancestral memories," asserting that there is left in every modern man some relics or embers of those predatory instincts by which our primitive fathers kept themselves alive. This "atavistic" theory, equally applicable to many other forms of sport and play, asserts that we now do for pleasure what we once did as a necessity. Angling is certainly as favorable an example as any that could be chosen, because the original element of necessity, the securing of food, is here submerged out of sight, and the method or technique is greatly enhanced in importance. One knows not a few fishermen who will not eat the fish they have caught, and who feel obliged after every trip to the stream to make another journey for the distribution of their catch among their friends. (When such men say that the taking of fish for the mere sake of fish is a small part of their sport, we ought to believe them.) Consider, too, how the sportsman multiplies unnecessary difficulties. If the capture of trout were his main purpose, then dynamite and the net should be his tools; but instead of these brutal devices he uses the lightest tackle he can afford and is happiest of all when he is risking a precious rod—worth a week's income to him and made by a week's toil at the bench—against a fish that weighs a pound for each of its ounces.

Accepting for the moment this theory that our delight in fishing is largely atavistic, we are able to estimate the distance that has been covered in the history of angling. It can be measured roughly by observing the difference between the fishing methods used by American Indians in the Nipigon river region, while getting in their winter supplies, and the technique of some sportsman on the same stream. The Indian uses a throw-line stout enough to hold a man-eating shark; the sportsman, casting for ouananiche that often weigh ten pounds, uses a rod of nine or ten ounces, a leader almost as thin and diaphanous as it can be drawn, a line of tapered silk, and a lure scarcely larger than a house-fly. This he does to improve his sport, for he finds that he enjoys fishing the more in proportion as he gives the fish a fighting chance, or rather as he increases the demands upon his own skill and resource.

The fisherman who fishes merely for a "mess" is of course exactly on a level with the pot-hunter, and must not be regarded as a sportsman at all. As Gervase Markham said rather brilliantly more than three hundred years ago, "The angler must entice, not command his reward, and that which is worth millions to his contentment another may buy for a groat in the market." But should this be taken to mean that the true sportsman does not care whether he catches fish? One has heard good anglers assert such indifference, but one ought never to believe them. Every sport, like every business and profession, has a certain number of commonplaces of this kind that come readily to the lips but seldom into the mind. This is merely one of the things that anglers say. I do not mean to suggest that it is in the slightest degree canting or hypocritical, for I think, rather, that it is merely the closest approach to the truth that they can make in talking to ignorant or unsympathetic persons. The truth they try to convey is that even when they catch no fish their expeditions are fully recompensed in other ways, that they get by far the more important part of what they go out for even when they return with empty creels. On this important topic we have the word of "Dame Juliana Berners" herself, whom many anglers echo without ever having heard her dubious name. If it turns out that the angler comes home empty-handed "because there be nought in the water," yet at the least, says she, "he hath his wholesome walk and merry at his ease, and a sweet air of the sweet savor of the mead flowers, that maketh him hungry. He heareth the melodious harmony of fowls. He seeth the young swans, herons, ducks, coots, and many other fowls with their broods. . . . Also, whoso will use the game of angling, he must rise early, which thing is profitable to a man in this wise, that is, to wit, most to the heal of his soul. For it shall cause him to be holy, and to the heal of his body, for it shall cause him to be whole. Also to the increase of his goods, for it shall make him rich. Thus have I proved in my intent that the disport and game of angling is the very mean and cause that induceth a man into a merry spirit, which maketh a flowering age and a long."

So much may be said, then, either to or by the man who returns with an empty basket, and it is a good deal; but Dame Juliana emphatically admits that the taking of fish is what makes his cup run over. "If the angler take fish," she says, "surely there is no man merrier in his spirit than he." Certainly it is a good sport, and a valuable training for life, that can teach a man to enjoy defeat without weakening his zest for victory.

Another explanation often made of the charm of fishing is that it provides escape or release from the pressure of modern life; and although somewhat too

THREAD OF THE RIVER

much has been made in recent years of the furious pace of our business and professional careers, we may allow that there is truth in this theory also. Good fishing, strenuous as it usually is in its higher branches, does certainly provide a sudden and refreshing change to the man who was toiling yesterday in Wall or Threadneedle Street. No sooner does he feel the cool pressure of the ripples against his waders than all customary thoughts slip from him, floating away down the stream before his first cast goes up. Senses and instincts long disused come into play. Odors, sounds, lights and shadows and motions, muscular strains, changes of temperature, flood all at once in upon him, stirring his oldest memories, blurring his latest cares. He seems to stand outside himself, and he looks back upon the man who was yesterday called by his name with fading comprehension and growing commiseration. Only for a fleeting instant now and then, however, does he think of that poor creature at all, for every nerve and muscle and sense is occupied, every faculty of his mind is at work upon what seem for the time far more important matters. What flies to choose, considering the season and time of day and color of water? What cast to use, in his position under trees, or at the end of a narrow pool, or behind a mid-stream rock? How to time the strike, according to all the hundred factors entering into that problem? How to play a large trout, too heavy for rod and leader, that bores and sulks

THY ROD AND THY CREEL

or makes off down the stream like a Cross-Continental Express, or else "springs from the deep and tries aërial ways." When to check and when to let him run, when and how to net him in swift water, and when to derrick him incontinently ashore, be the cost to pride and tackle what it may—these, and a thousand other matters, never forgetting the difficulty to feet just come from city pavements of keeping their hold on rocks sloping like toboggan-slides or rounded like footballs, and all of them covered with millennial moss over which swift water is running mid-thigh deep, are usually found sufficient to postpone all anxious thoughts about the condition of the Stock Market or next Sunday's sermon or even the unwritten book-review three months overdue.

It has been observed that when a man is engaged in a "business deal" he smokes his pipe smoothly and continuously from match to white ash; that when he is writing ordinary prose he has to relight once in five minutes; that for poetical composition the average time between match and match is two minutes and a half; but that a trout-fisher in action smokes matches almost exclusively. (And the difficulty of getting at and striking those matches! For if he lets the line float idly down-stream during the operation then he gets, and loses, the best rise of the morning just when his rod-hand is slapping and fumbling on its errand. Or he may gather in the line, transfer it together with the rod to the left hand, and then go searching here and there with wet fingers among the debris of last year's pockets, finding plenty of tangled leaders and rusty hooks and stray angle-worms, but no match. At last, in desperation with the black flies and smokelessness, the angler decides that his matches must have crawled somehow into his creel. This, therefore, he jerks impatiently from back to front—and then his net falls into the water. At such a juncture almost anything may happen, but let us suppose that he first slaps wildly at the mosquito whose deserts have fallen far into arrears and then plunges after his net, intending to wet only his arm but losing his balance and falling headlong. And then, of course, after struggling to his feet, he will reach for the handkerchief in his hip-pocket and will find therein his little cache of matches—thoroughly water-logged, a mass of sticky sulphur.)

Clearly, there is some truth in this "escape" theory. One can play the piano while thinking of the morning's mail, or one can watch a baseball game while planning a bank-robbery, but in order to fish successfully, at any rate for the nobler species, one must give one's whole attention to the sport in hand. And this is the reason why a trout-rod is the best magician's wand for exorcising the ghosts of care. This is the truth that lies behind that *Angler's Song* made famous by Walton and set to a good tune by Henry Lawes:

THY ROD AND THY CREEL

Man's life is but vain,
For 'tis subject to pain
And sorrow, and short as a bubble;
'Tis a hodge-podge of business and money and care
And care and money and trouble.
But we'll take no care
When the weather proves fair,
Nor will we vex now though it rain;
We'll banish all sorrow
And sing till tomorrow
And angle and angle again.

We must not expect too much, however, of any single theory, and this one will not explain all, or half, of the delights of angling. For it must not be ignored, in the first place, that we enjoy fishing not for negative reasons alone but for several positive ones—not only for what it enables us to forget but for what it makes us remember. The escape theory, moreover, does not go far toward explaining the passion for the sport to be observed in all normal and well-constituted boys. I am quite sure, for example, that when I myself, at the age of eight or nine, used to carry my tin bucket, my hazel rod, and my bent pin on the end of a length of wrapping string down to Kent's creek —an obscure and dismal tributary of the Rock River in Illinois—and there sat through the blaze of many an August afternoon, now and then pulling up a three-

THREAD OF THE RIVER

inch perch or bull-head which I carefully placed in the tin bucket for purposes of exhibition, I was not actuated by any desire to escape from carking care. And yet those were almost perfect fishing days. I have made some improvements in paraphernalia, perhaps even in technique, since then, and I have fished in a good many more famous waters, but yet I think those days were almost as good as any that have followed in the one important respect that they gave me the angler's special kind of pleasure. It seems necessary, therefore, to look further for the sources of that pleasure, or rather to add others to those already named.

One of these is the element of uncertainty always present in the sport of angling so long as it remains a sport. I have fished in the late season in Nova Scotia when the trout were so "schooled up" that one drew in at least one fish of a pound or more at almost every cast. That was more like work than play. Also I have talked with fishermen, and have read the writings of others, who feel that they have quite eliminated the element of chance from their fishing. Weather conditions, height of water, season of the year, popularity of streams, whims and caprices and conflicting engagements of the trout themselves, make no difference to these gentry: they lay their calculations, adjust themselves to circumstances and always catch fish—presumably all they want. My own attitude toward these anglers, if they can be called that, is respectful but quite unmixed with envy. It would be pleasant to have their knowledge and skill, of course, but one would not like to know that one had it. To my thinking there is something even vulgar in such self-confidence, and it seems to me almost as ugly in an angler as it would be in a lover. The man who is absolutely certain that he can catch trout under any and all conditions has no longer any good reason that I can see for doing so. He has ceased to be a sportsman and has decayed into a mere professional fish-catcher. Henceforth he might as well buy his trout from his butcher and leave the streams to those who can still enjoy them.

In my own humbler encounters with *salvelinus fontinalis* there has always been, I am glad to say, a very large element of chance and uncertainty, and if I may judge from the progress thus far made and the distance there is yet to go I think there always will be. I have travelled two hundred miles by train and automobile and wagon to get at a famous river at the best season, only to find the spring freshets over all the banks and the trout swimming high among the alder branches. I have walked ten miles up a mountain-side to fish a series of pools which had held many good trout a month before—and have found those pools bone-dry. (The experts mentioned above would have been quite undismayed by these apparently untoward circumstances, but to me they were daunting; they took their place among the ten thousand disappointments and minor catastrophes that keep the amateur angler continually in mind of the fact that this is an imperfect world—and a world, therefore, in which there is some sport left.) I have fished with might and main when all the conditions—tackle, time of day, season, water, cover—were, or seemed, exactly right, and have caught exactly nothing. Who has not? Also I have fished when most of these conditions seemed to my thinking wrong, and have caught as many trout as were good for me. Again, what angler has not? Instead of gathering from such experiences a sense of invincible power, I find that the more I fish for trout the more uncertain I am what they will do under given circumstances, the more convinced I am that they are mysterious creatures and their ways past our finding out. I do not even know on what grounds a trout accepts, or rejects, an artificial fly—whether in accepting it he takes it for a natural fly or merely for something unspecified that might possibly be digestible and is apparently trying to get away. I do not know whether he pays most attention—or any—to the color, the shape, or the size of the lures we put above him, although I suspect that size and motion mean more to him than other things. Of course there are many authorities on the shelf and elsewhere who are ready to enlighten me on all these matters and many others of

THY ROD AND THY CREEL

the same nature. My difficulty is that the opinions of the authorities conflict and cancel one another out, leaving me to my own observation and judgment.

And for all this one should be thankful. Humanly speaking, omniscience and omnipotence are simply fatal to sport. The uncertainty that most of us find in trout-fishing is one of its most obvious charms; it draws us back to running water every April that the gods allot us and keeps us waving old age away with a rod and a looping line. Angling is like one of those everlasting puzzles that we seem to solve again and again, each time we solve them forgetting the solutions or finding that they will not work a second time. At every cast of the line, every time that our flies flutter down to the water, there is a vast range of possible happenings before us, extending all the way from absolute zero—or even from any conceivable minus quantity, such as that representing a snag or a broken leader or a smashed tip—up to a sudden circling weight, a leaping beam of light, a battle royal, and a two-foot rainbow prone on the moss. To send those feathers fluttering down the air, to see them settle gently as the eyelashes of a child that is falling asleep, to watch them come slowly back, surveyed from below by rapacious eyes, and all the while to be alert in body and mind and quiet at heart—this, to a good many men whose intelligence none of us would care to gainsay, is one of the more absorbing occupations that life affords. Childish, shall we call it, or boyish at the best? It can stir and hold men who have known most other kinds of conflict, who have won the world's honors, and who know quite well that the keenest and most enduring satisfactions are those of the mind. Indeed, the assertion may be ventured that the more highly organized a man is the more he is likely to enjoy angling of the highest sort. The more he knows about action, the more this active and meditative sport will allure him. The greater his knowledge of men and books, the greater will be his delight in the mysteries of the stream.

Uncertainties of many kinds surround the angler at every turn, so that even when most skilful he is still beset by "misgivings of a creature moving about in worlds not realized." In the purchase of a trout-rod—unless he be one of those extremely cautious persons who distrust all woods and canes and put their faith in nothing but steel—what hazards he runs of flaws that lurk unseen, of tops too whippy or too stiff, of butts that never fit the hand. A poor choice of a reel, or a grain of sand in that reel after it is purchased, may determine the outcome of some battle to be remembered all the rest of his days with groanings of spirit. A line that tapers too much or too little, a leader too fine or too heavy, a fly too large—but never, I think, a fly too small—loses him that epochal trout, object of his happiest dreams, that might have been the main trophy of his angling career. But worse than these, for these are things that a man may control in some degree if he be omniscient and a millionaire, are the rocks that roll at crucial moments, the logs and sunken tree-tops and rock-pockets in which a hooked trout can lie hidden for months at a time, the trees that intervene between the angler and the pool, and the trees that do *not* intervene. All that the angler can expect with perfect confidence is the unexpected; all that he can certainly foresee and try to provide for is the unforeseen. Fishing for trout, I have often thought, is a little more like life than actual living is. Or rather, it is life with its moments of anguish and ecstasy crowded more closely together than they commonly are in other sorts of experience—life heightened and intensified by the spirit of play, and fortune not controlled but tempted, challenged, sometimes conquered. Here too there is a brief bitterness in defeat and elation in victory, but these emotions do not exact the expense of spirit that we must pay down in other contests. It is true that the memory of a thrilling capture may glow in the mind for many years, for a long life time, and also that the loss of a good fish is not soon forgotten. Dean Swift wrote to Alexander Pope: "I remember when I was a little boy, I felt a great fish at the end of my line, which I drew up almost to the ground, but it dropped in, and the disappointment vexes me to this day." Yes, no doubt;

THREAD OF THE RIVER

for every angler has a hundred memories of such "great fish"; but I do not think that this experience, grievous though it was at the time, can have been the exciting cause of Dean Swift's settled gloom. He may have worked it into his conviction that all the world was against him, that nothing he did ever prospered, that life was decidedly not worth living, but that would have been because he had a morbid appetite for misery which could digest almost anything. Such memories, even when they are very numerous, do not amount in normal minds to a permanent sorrow, partly because they are balanced by as many recollections of success and more because they are all surrounded and suffused by the atmosphere of play. Tragic events may occur in comedy, and often do, but they are never allowed to have tragic effect.

I think, then, that we must accept the uncertainty of angling as one of the main sources or phases of its charm. The angler can never count upon his prize from the instant of the strike until the fish is finally basketed—no, nor even then; for there are still keepers and game-wardens to be reckoned with, creels are sometimes left unlatched and empty their contents back into rivers, captured trout are as acceptable as any to minks and herons and also to house cats. In fact, the fisherman may sit back and take his ease only when he sees his fish steaming before him on a dinner plate. —And then it may be unfit to eat.

III

WHAT seems to me the primary and most enduring source of the angler's happiness has already been mentioned. This, in a word, is wild nature—a very ancient word which has been grossly sentimentalized of late, and is soiled with all ignoble use, but which must still serve our turn. Every good angler will have his notion of what I mean by it—a notion that will certainly over-lap my own without being exactly coincident with it—and I believe that if he could analyze all the many elements of his pleasure in fishing he would find that this one predominates. As a rule, and quite properly, he does not analyze them, being too much occupied with what seem for the time more important considerations. His impressions come to him, as William James says the first experiences of life come to an infant, in a vast humming and buzzing confusion. Nevertheless, for nine good anglers out of ten, although nearly the same number would probably deny it, the sights and sounds and odors that surround the fisherman are more than the fishing. Set one of them to angling in an indoor swimming pool well stocked with three-pounders, and the most dubious will admit the truth of what I say.

THREAD OF THE RIVER

Angling is of course by no means the only sport of which this may be said, let any grown American who enjoyed a normal boyhood think back far enough through the years and he will find that all his recollections of his early out-door games are entangled with faint or vivid memories of weather and of seasons. Peg-tops and top-spinning are associated with the end of winter, marbles with earliest spring, kite-flying with June and July, baseball with the blazing days of August, and the thought of football comes mingled with colors of flying leaves and smoke of autumnal bonfires. Skating, tobogganing, snowshoeing, skiing, bring other associations not less vivid, and the still earlier games of childhood such as prisoner's base, pull-away, and hide-and-go-seek are even more heavily charged with memories of nature. There must be a million Americans living today who can recall the time when nutting was a festival that took us every October into the enchanted woods. We did not come back from those excursions in farm-carts and buckboards quite the same boys and girls that we were when we set out. Certain things were decided for us once and for all by influences of which we were scarcely aware—by the odors of decaying foliage, by the patterns of gold against the blue, by the twirling fall of a leaf. We may think that we have forgotten all these things, but the sight of a single flaming maple or even some vaguely related strain of music brings them back, and it would require half of an eternity to wear away the gold of those high hickories from our thoughts. All day long we were climbing trees, throwing sticks, gathering fallen nuts, and the closest observation would not have discovered that we paid a moment's attention to the banners of autumn about us, and yet today we discover this fine deposit in the cells of memory—whisper of ferns, scents, blue of the asters that withered three decades ago, gold of the leaves that have gone back into sod and climbed again into trees and flowers.

What can all this mean, if not that some part, apparently a large one, of our enjoyment in those old games and excursions was derived, although we did not know it, from natural influences? We must have seen those immense cities of cloud, splendidly domed and turreted, that loomed above the baseball diamond, and seen them with strange intensity, while we thought we were wholly occupied with watching the ball, else they would not come so vividly back to us now. The chill of evening and approaching winter, cold airs and odors of burning leaves and of wood-smoke, that used to creep or flow across the field during the last minutes of a football game, must have been felt most keenly at the time in the midst of all our rough-and-tumble, or else they would not now lie waiting for us in the darkened rooms of memory whenever we turn the keys in those old wards. No doubt it was the "subliminal mind" that snatched up and stored these treasures while all the conscious attention was earnestly trained upon the game, but that does not lessen their potency or dim their present charm. The game itself, even the mighty effort to win or to excel in that game, occupied the center of attention, but quite other things, having no apparent relation to the game, were seen, so to speak, with the more sensitive outer fringes of the retina and recorded indelibly.

Now there is no reason to suppose that this faculty of gathering impressions from fields outside the focus of attention is peculiar to childhood. We know that it is not. Considered all together, these impressions are more important to feeling than sport itself; they compose the nimbus or aureole through which the sportsman sees his game, whatever it may be, and only by reference to them can we explain how it happens that thousands of intelligent men derive from sport somewhat the same satisfactions that others do from art and religion.

What is the difference in attitude toward the game of golf between an ignorant and unimaginative spectator and an expert player? To the former it consists entirely in knocking a little hard ball here and there over the grass until it rolls finally into a hole, after which it is extracted and knocked some more—a sufficiently dull and childish pastime. To the skilful player it is ten thousand other things, such as a delight and a despair, schooling in accuracy of mind and body and in self-control, opportunity for self-conquest. He sees it not baldly and barely but as a multiple thing; he thinks of it in connection with all its rich connotations and in terms of a million memories stored away in nerves and muscles and brain. The most useful of these memories for practical purposes are those that preserve successful stances and strokes, bodily motions and balances, but the most important to his pleasure in the game are those that seem secondary or even unrelated to the sport. Say the word "golf" to him and he is as likely as not to smell the dewy grass just warmed by the sun of early morning, to feel the firm soft sod of the green under foot, to see a spot of brightness edged by shadow lifting against a summer cloud, or to hear the drone of friendly voices chaffing in the locker-room. He cares no more for merely knocking a small white ball about than any other sensible man, but he loves the game of golf—loves it in its entirety, somewhat as one loves a woman, not solely or chiefly because she has blue eyes.

Something like this may be said of all out-door sports, but of none more emphatically than of angling. There are people in the world who see nothing in the angler's occupation but tedium, laziness, cruelty, and lies—or, as some wiseacre has phrased it, "a fly at one end of a line and a fool at the other." Peace be

THREAD OF THE RIVER

to all such, and a better way—if they can find it—of spending their leisure time, more human, more humane, more fit for an honest man. Say "fishing" to the angler, however, or mention any one of the tools of his sport, and you call up more memories than could be named in a year—memories of sunny days and foul, of virgin dawns and serene nightfalls, of bending rods, leaping gold and crimson, rippling green, of camp fires far and near, of talk and of silence and of friends. Into his mental pictures of angling he has painted the sky, the trees, the ferns and moss, most of all, the water, and the colors run. Probably there is no other sport that carries one so far toward the secret heart of nature as angling does. This is to say that the memories of nature laid away by the angler are richer, more vivid and more various, than those acquired in other sports.—If one were disposed to follow this line of argument a little further he might succeed in proving what every angler knows, that fishing is the finest sport in the world. But anglers are seldom argumentative. They prefer to make their assertions and have done. Furthermore, they are never eager for converts, at any rate in our time, feeling more than satisfied with the number of fishermen they find on the stream at dawn of opening day. Therefore they may sometimes say that angling is the best of sports, but they seldom attempt to prove it.

Wild nature, as I have said, is the most important,

as it is also the most enduring source of the angler's pleasure, and the phase of nature with which he is most concerned is the most beautiful, mysterious, and fascinating of all—wild water. Any one who has once seen and felt the amazing loveliness of swiftly running water, whether in the meadow brook or the mountain torrent, whether lustrous under leaves or flashing to the open sky, can understand without elaborate explanation the charm that lures and holds the angler. He has fallen under a spell that has been known in all ages and has been symbolized in many a legend of Sirens, Loreleis, Undines, and other water-witches. He is bemused by the babble of water, by the fragrance and song of it, by its broken and reflected and piercing and shimmering lights, by its constant change on the surface of its deep changelessness, and most of all by its motion. To his ears the stream sings in a hundred voices low and high, intermittent or continuous, and he can separate these voices and hear what each is saying as a conductor unravels the total harmony of his orchestra and finds the throbbing of a single string. To his eyes the stream brings glitter, ever-changing hues, curves of inimitable and never-failing grace, and the magical effect of motion in the midst of a stable landscape—the leaping white jet of life. And this beauty, moreover, is always mysterious to him, meaning something beyond what it shows and says; and after he has studied it for a life time it is not less mysterious but more so, more strange and so more alluring. It is this mystery and challenging strangeness that the angler sets his will and wit to explore. Standing in one element, he invades another, striving to search it thoroughly. With a fifty-foot finger of bamboo and silk and gut he probes the deeps and the shallows, feels along the riffles, glides slowly out into bays of glitter, striving toward and almost attaining a sixth sense, trying to surprise the water's innermost secret law.—But this, of course, he will never do. In other arts and crafts, and even in a few sports, we can distinguish the three stages of apprentice, journeyman, and master; but in angling few ever pass beyond apprenticeship, and masters there are none.

Wild water—how it draws us back to itself from our boyhood to our oldest age, and lures us on and on, down and down, as though just beyond each bend lay the answers to all our questionings and the goal of all our hopes. It draws and lures us by an infinite variety. No two stretches of any living brook are the same or similar to a seeing eye, and no square foot of it is the same for two moments together. Depth, color, bottom, angle of light from above and from below, rapidity of current, speed and size of ripples, vagaries of breeze and calm, time of day, season of the year—all of these and a thousand other factors and influences playing together and into one another make any wayside brook more bewilderingly various than anything short of a lifelong study can teach one to realize. In streams well supplied with rocks and boulders standing up from the surface there is, in addition all the grace of water-curves never-ending, looping long and far, shaping streams within the stream, edged and flecked with foam. Where trees grow near there is added the dappling of light and shade, slumbrous when the breeze is still and dancing when the boughs are set aswing.

But the brook is not for the eye alone; it is the string of a mighty violin, stretched between the mountains and the sea. And it has a great gamut, from the broad rumbling bass of the main current rounding a granite boulder to the tiny trebles of little ripples sparkling pizzicato in the shallows. Where the stream flows wide over gravel beds there are numberless singers blending their tones like so many leaves in a tree, but where it narrows and bores between rocky walls the voices crowd together in one vague shout. Comes a fall, and the shout deepens to a roar, overlaid by faint screams and splashings and by tones that sound in desolate places like those of the human voice calling from far away. Below the fall there is heard, underneath the sound of steady onrush, a half-drowned subaqueous grumbling from the under-tow as of some giant tossing there, and a clamor of somersaulting currents that boil upward and break outward into the day. Every bubble of the thousands bursting here adds its particle to the tumult, and the long sigh of the current slipping past reeds at the stream's edge is added also. One hundred feet farther down the water quiets into a pool. All the uproar becomes an echo, then a memory. There is only the faint ruffling of the breeze on the backs of the ripples. But at the sill of the pool a stickle begins; this grows to a water-slide; then comes a fallen tree through whose branches the stream washes and gurgles in muted tones. After that, once more there is the broad deep rumbling of the main current and all the repertoire is played over again, though never in the same order or with exact repetition of any part. Usually, too, more than one variety of stream-song is heard at the same moment. The string is double-stopped.

Thomas Hardy somewhere says that an English peasant who has been brought up among trees can tell where he is in a familiar countryside on the darkest night, merely by the sound of the wind among the leaves, which varies widely from one species to another. However this may be, it is certain that an experienced trout-fisher can guide himself fairly well in night-fishing by the sound of the water alone; and in the daytime he has always some idea of the stretches ahead of him before he rounds a bend. Instinctively, he estimates the depth of a pool and the strength of a current almost as much by the ear as by the eye, and the sounds of the water suggest to him many devices, warn him that rocks will roll or that the trout are

THY ROD AND THY CREEL

lying against the farther bank. He hears and analyzes a hundred signals in the hurl of the water of which he is never consciously aware.

What can a man desire more when standing knee-deep in a mountain river, rod in hand, with trout on the rise? Here he has earth and air and sky before him, strangely interfused and woven into one element. The brook runs over the bones of the planet and carries the sky on its back, so that it is a complete world, and one who gazes into this crystal long and steadily will find there not food and drink only but work and play, patience and excitement, knowledge and wisdom, fact and dream. Here indeed is one of the forms of nature that pass into our moods with tranquil restoration. Either the stream teaches or else it recalls to mind some of the deeper truths that are seldom thought of but are good to know. Consider, for example, the almost universal belief—universal, at any rate, in the western world—that every one desires to live forever, preserving his own individuality forever intact. What has the stream to say about that matter? Well, we see that it is moving steadily, as swiftly as possible and by the shortest possible course, toward the sea and the merging of its tiny self into a vastly greater. What sort of water is it that "lives forever" and preserves its identity intact? The stagnant pool, mantled with obscene scum and foul with all forms of death.—Deeper teachings than this the stream has for

THREAD OF THE RIVER

us—as, how to mingle freedom with restraint and law with liberty. It keeps pace with us, or rather it runs on before. In its slender source far up the mountain there was already a sure and glad foreknowledge of the end. One who could understand wild water—as no man ever will—would be far on the road to understanding all things, so full it is of symbols and correspondencies with our lives; and it may be a dim realization of this that brings us back to the stream's side whenever we can get there, that keeps us bending for hour after hour over bridges, that makes the heart leap when we see from a passing train the white feather of a brook on a distant hillside, and that holds us awake in the night listening to the voice of a river rushing through darkness. That river is the metaphor of time to us, and we are children of Time. It rushes toward the sea of oblivion, as we do. It would linger if it could in this pool, in that eddy, under such a bending elm, but a stronger need and wish draws it down, forever down, toward its swaying and softly breathing rest.

Down and down, forever down. Imagination faints in the effort to realize how long it has been falling. The angler comes to a gorge worn hundreds of feet deep in solid rock by nothing but the everlasting trample of tiny water-drops. He casts his flies over huge circular pools of granite scooped by the slow gyration of pebbles and sand during years hardly to be expressed by arithmetic. Numberless pools such as

THY ROD AND THY CREEL

these are to be seen in the Rocky Mountains, fifty feet deep and as many in diameter, where the great trout swim in a liquid emerald. "Earth has not anything to show more fair." Neither is there anything to be seen on this side of the Pearly Gates more lovely than the grottoes and caverns carved by flowing water in a mountain's flank, banked with moss and overhung by ferns. The boulders strewn up and down such rivers have a more savage grandeur than boulders to be seen elsewhere, as though they had learned nobility from the song of the water round them. The fisherman comes to a huge fallen crag rising thirty feet or more above the stream and commanding a long vista of checkered shade and shine, leaping foam and trembling sun-dazzle, and the sun may go down upon him while he sits there, his tackle at his feet. Or he finds small crevices in the rocky bed where the water is a flowing topaz that checks the swing of his wrist almost in mid-cast by its beauty, and many a pool that must contain good trout he walks round without throwing a line, because it seems too perfect for him to profane even by the fluttering of a tuft of feathers. He need not be superstitious, or even much of a scholar, to feel that such places are sanctified by some tutelary spirit or local goddess such as Milton's youths invoked:

Sabrina fair,
Listen where thou art sitting

THREAD OF THE RIVER

Under the glassy, cool, translucent wave,
In twisted braids of lilies knitting
The loose train of thine amber-dropping hair.

Wild water left to itself can never fail to be beautiful, and it will not endure the slightest ugliness about it. This is true not only of the mountain river but of the meadow brook as well, flowing almost mute among reeds and grasses and under willow trees. There are stretches of the upper Thames, where it winds among the level lands that William Morris loved and flows twenty miles to make five of headway, that are as beautiful in their July coloring as anything to be seen in high Switzerland. The little Musketaquid also, that steals through Concord with so slow a tread that Hawthorne was for three weeks in doubt which way it flows, has nothing to learn in the lore of rivers. Indeed, almost any nameless rivulet creeping from root to tussock in a New England pasture reveals all the range of loveliness to be seen in the Amazon from source to mouth, if only one has the patience and skill to find it.

IV

I HAVE tried to show that angling owes much of its charm to the scenes in which it is practised. If this is now admitted, I may proceed to suggest that we of the present day enjoy angling more keenly than it has ever been enjoyed before. It can be proved in the pages of Ælian, to be sure, that fishing with the fly was known to the ancients, and fly-fishing has always been fishing for pleasure. On the other hand, if there is anything whatever in the "argument from silence," it seems doubtful whether any large number of persons had quite our modern feeling for nature before the beginning of the eighteenth century. But we have just seen that our present delight in fishing is in some large measure due to this same feeling for nature. Does it not seem to follow that angling as we know it, or rather as we feel about it, is a modern sport?

I can see the over-worked reviewer, who has time to read only a sentence or two of any book and no time to understand even those, seize his typewriter at this point and convict me of ignorance in a few crisp words. Yet I really do know quite well that angling of some sort is one of the most ancient of human occupations, and I am aware that a dozen classics of the sport were

THREAD OF THE RIVER

written before the date I have mentioned. It is of modern angling that I speak here, and I would suggest that this differs somewhat in technique and profoundly in total atmosphere from the angling described by Oppian, Ælian, Gaston Phœbus, Dame Juliana, Gervase Markham, John Dennys, Thomas Barker, Richard Franck, Charles Cotton, and Izaak Walton. To cross out Walton himself, or rather to set a barrier between us and the man who has been so often called the Father of Angling, is perhaps an audacious thing to do, but I hazard the guess that although he probably enjoyed his fishing as much as we do he enjoyed it differently and for different reasons. How mild and domestic is that scene between Piscator and Venator with which he opens his book! He is footing up Tottenham Hill toward Ware on the Lea, we remember. (Dear old fellow; he always had to walk all the way to his fishing—a matter of twenty miles it was on the expedition in question—and this must have shortened his time by the stream not a little when he had passed beyond his three-score and ten.) Well, the Lea flowed down into London then as it does now. It is today the mildest of pastoral waters, and it can never have been a wild stream even in the days when King Alfred deflected its current to maroon the boats of the Danes. There is, in fact, no feeling for the wilderness in Walton, or for that matter in Charles Cotton, who nevertheless fished in a much more romantic region.

THY ROD AND THY CREEL

Many other excellent things there are in him, but without this he does not quite qualify as the parent of us all.

If one were asked to name an individual earlier than the eighteenth century who probably felt about angling somewhat as we do, one could not do better than to cite the poet and scholar and courtier Francis Petrarch. It is true that he mentions his angling seldom and makes little of it in the account; but on the other hand, he lived almost alone for several years in one of the wildest scenes in Europe, just where the River Sorgue comes rushing full-grown from a mountain's side. We know from his account that there were noble trout in the Sorgue in the fourteenth century. I have seen a few there that might well have been growing ever since his time.

Any modern angler who makes the long journey out from Avignon and sees the superb stream beside which Petrarch lived so long with the shout of the headlong waters in his ears all night and day, will see that he must have been, in at least one important respect, a man of our own kind; but the people of his own century regarded him with an amazement not unlike that of the women who pointed at Dante as he moved through the streets, saying "There goes the man who has been to Hell." The ancient Romans themselves had felt that there was something supernatural about the place, and had expressed their feeling by imagining a guardian spirit to rule over it. Early Christians, according to their custom, had changed the Roman god into a dragon, which became so troublesome that the Pope was finally obliged to send up a carefully chosen holy man to drive him away. Seven centuries later, but still a full generation before Chaucer sat down to write his *Canterbury Tales*, the young poet Petrarch came to Vaucluse and loitered in the moonlight, thumbed his Latin classics, wrote or planned most of his books, and fished for trout in the Sorgue. The devils that troubled him there were many, but he felt that he had imported them all from Avignon, Naples, and Rome. He saw nothing of the dragon, but he did see the glory of the Sorgue's green water as perhaps no man before his time had seen such things. He heard with a strange new delight the voices of the wilderness that terrified most of his contemporaries. He was happier in the Closed Valley than ever elsewhere in all his wide wanderings.

This may seem remote from my topic, but it is not. Petrarch showed by precept and example—and even in his life time he was one of the most famous men in Europe—that the wilderness is habitable not merely by ascetic saints but by a person of delicate nurture and refined tastes. He damned the city and the crowds and the fools thereof all the year round with the same heartiness that the modern angler feels chiefly at the beginning of April, and he did it with a splendor of vituperation that very few anglers can emulate. Whether for good or ill, and probably for both, he reversed the ancient notion that one grows crude and boorish in the country and wise in the city. He did much to revive the still more ancient belief that "the woods were God's first temples," and that "to him who in the love of Nature holds communion with her various forms she speaks a various language." This was an important service to anglers.

Innovations of thought and feeling made by such lonely pioneers as Petrarch, however, are often unfruitful, and even more frequently their influence is long postponed. Most of Petrarch's thought was immediately and enormously prolific, but his feeling for the wilderness had to be rediscovered and rephrased by writers such as Rousseau and painters such as Salvator Rosa before it could gain currency. This tiny trickle, helped out by many tributaries, began to form a rivulet about two hundred years ago, and in England, so that angling as we know it may be said to be about two centuries old.

Considered somewhat liberally as a sport with an atmosphere of its own, modern angling may owe as much to persons like Paul Sandby, the early watercolorist, whose names never appear in the manuals, as it does to Halford or Stewart. I suspect that it owes rather more to Sir Walter Scott, whom we cannot even claim as a "brother of the angle" than it does to Izaak Walton, for it was Scott who spread most widely broadcast the delight in "romantic" landscape, which before his time had been felt by comparatively few. James Thomson of *The Seasons*, who was too lazy to be a good angler but who had energy enough to write rather well about the sport, contributed his share toward the preparation, and so did Thomas Gray, who may never, so far as I know, have creeled a single fish. In the same category belong a score of German philosophers and critics and poets with whose names no angler need burden his memory, and also a dozen or more of "Deists," French and English, who taught that although supernatural revelation could no longer be credited yet we had still before us the open book of the streams and forests, by means of which we might proceed "through Nature to Nature's God."

These Deists of the eighteenth century, in their teaching that the study of nature and association with it is really a contemplation of divine truth, asserted a conviction the roots of which grope down to the beginnings of human thought. It was a revival, long postponed by Christian hostility, of the old idea, illustrated by the legends of Moses and Solon and Buddha and Numa Pompilius, that there is a kind of wisdom, the highest and deepest kind, that a man may gain only by dwelling alone in the wilderness, where the gods are accustomed to congregate. Deism said nothing of the gods, to be sure—they who were anciently supposed to converse directly with the truth-seeker—but it expressed the old conviction in its new language. This expression was vastly influential, and we are living still in the midst of its effects, but it did not produce—perhaps it could not produce in our energetic western world—lonely and passive seers like the Yogis of India. We have had only one Thoreau. One of its effects has been the acceleration of modern science; another, the deepening of our love for nature.

Father Izaak, although by no means a Deist, had unconsciously absorbed a good deal of this faith that nature is a sort of subsidiary revelation of the divine, and that is the underlying reason for the subtitle of his book—"The Contemplative Man's Recreation." What does "contemplation" mean to him? First of all, it means looking through and beyond the shows of things to the spirit that informs them. Also, it means quiet of mind and peace of heart, the whole man lying fallow for whatever seeds may sift down upon him from the hand of some unimaginable sower.

Izaak Walton lived his long life, as we must remember if we are to understand him, in times of constant turmoil, and he had need of every quieting message that the Lea and Itchen and Dove could whisper to him. England has had two periods of exceptional angling enthusiasm, if we may distinguish one epoch of sport from another in the history of a country in which sport is always enthusiastic—that which followed the uproar of the Civil Wars and that following the English aftermath of the French Revolution. The connection may be imaginary, but also it may be real, and may indicate the need we all feel after times of extreme stress to find our way back to basic and simple things. (Some of the most impassioned fishermen I have ever met in America have been men who served at the front in the Great War.) Many of us have lost even the shadowy faith of the Deists and their successors that nature is the symbol of "something far more deeply interfused," and this is certainly one of the most tragic losses that human minds have ever been called upon to endure, yet even for such bereaved and hopeless souls there is something left, some assurance that can neither be described nor explained, in the voice of summer streams. A man of our time who has thought his way through and out of all religions and philosophies, winning as reward only a dull despair, may still discover as he works his way up a mountain brook on a morning in May that his thought has taken a wrong trail somewhere far back in the years. The ferns seem to possess some knowledge for which he has not allowed, and the stream has a meaning which he has ignored.

But this water may seem a little too deep for our waders. I can suggest nearly all that I have been trying to say explicitly in terms of the good word "leisure," which for the most part we misunderstand and grossly misuse. Angling is leisure—that is, an activity engaged in for its own sake. It induces in the western man, who must be lured away from his strenuosity by specious devices, a leisure of mood and mind which may do him some deeper good than earning him a basket of fish, and in which he may possibly learn something for his lasting good. At the least, it withdraws thousands of men for a few days of every year from the frenzy of their going and getting—and once they are thus withdrawn, who knows what doubts may occur to them concerning the value of their former activities, what questions that go to the roots of their daily lives, what thoughts that may spring up into a fairer and happier living?

We may see this process going on while watching the men about the fires of fishing camps in the evenings. Nothing in human nature is much more disheartening than the spectacle of the low-bred and coarse-minded Babbitt just arrived in camp, manumitted for the customary fortnight from the office chair, and trying at first to carry on in the wilderness with the same methods of shoving and elbowing that serve him so well in the city. The unwonted liberty of the forest he misinterprets as license to do as he pleases. He unlimbers his most revolting language and his foulest stories at the same time that he unpacks his

THREAD OF THE RIVER

still viler bootleg liquor; he builds fires recklessly and does not extinguish them; he throws his lighted matches into whatever tinder the woods contain; he does not so much catch fish as slay them. In general, he makes himself about as agreeable and welcome in the camp as a rattlesnake might be on its first arrival. But consider this same man a week later. His stories have all been told; he has come to suspect that his more lurid expletives do not harmonize with the surroundings, or that they are not duly appreciated; his bottles have all floated down the stream as "dead soldiers"; some vigorous guide has conveyed to him the elementary notions about the handling of fire. On the whole, he is a quieter man. One must not call him a thoughtful one, but at least he is beginning to have doubts. A spark disturbs his clod. If only he had two years before him instead of a pitiful week, he might learn enough to last him.

V

GOOD fishermen, of course, never stand in need of such training in the elementary decencies. They train others. I could wish that the praise of anglers, which is most voluminous and enthusiastic, had not come in quite such large part from anglers themselves, although of course it had to come from some one and they are the only persons who are fully cognizant of the facts. We may judge what Dame Juliana thought of them from the words in which she warns off the unworthy: "And for by cause that this present treatyse sholde not come to the hondys of eche ydle persone whyche wolde desire it yf it were emprynted allone by itself and put in a lytyll plaunflet, therefore have I compylyd it in a greter volume of dyverse bokys concernynge to gentyll and noble men. To the intente that the forsayd ydle persones whych scholde have but lytyll mesure in the sayde dysporte of fysshynge sholde not by this meane utterly dystroye it." Izaak Walton, who certainly knew a good man when he saw one, never tired of praising anglers and insisting, in spite of all report and even appearance to the contrary, that they are "honest men." In his Epistle Dedicatory he remarks that "there be now many men

THREAD OF THE RIVER

of great wisdom, learning, and experience, which love and practise this art." Writing of Dr. Alexander Nowel, Walton is proud to record that he was wont "to bestow a tenth part of his revenue, and usually all his fish, amongst the poor that inhabited near to those rivers in which it was caught; and at his return home to his house he would praise God he had spent that day free from worldly trouble, both harmlessly and in a recreation that became a Churchman. And this good man was well content that posterity should know he was an angler, as may appear by his picture, in which he is drawn leaning on a desk with his Bible before him, and on one hand of him his lines, hooks, and other tackling lying in a round, and on his other hand are his angle-rods of several sorts."

Walton always contrives to convey an effect of charm into every picture of an angler he draws. Here, for example, is a passage about the poet Francis Quarles which, although somewhat too florid for a severe taste, has much of his quality: "He in a Sommers morning (about that howre when the great eye of Heaven first opens it selfe to give light to us Mortals) walking a gentle pace towards a Brooke (whose Spring-head was not far distant from his peacefull Habitation) fitted with Angle, Lines, and Flyes: Flyes proper for that season (being the fruitfull Month of May) intending all diligence to beguile the timorous Trout (with which the watry element abounded) observed a more than usuall Concourse of Shepheards all bending their steps toward a pleasant Meadow."

The total effect of Walton's several passages in this vein is that anglers are distinctly superior to the common run of men, and that they are notable, in particular, for their piety, their powers of contemplation, their honesty, their energy, and their gentleness. I shall have nothing to say about the exceptional piety of fishermen, beyond the passing and perhaps not very significant remark that the brotherhood assays a surprising proportion of clergymen, for the "language" I have heard from them in various parts of the world at times when last leaders have been snapped in two, when favorite flies have been caught and held out of reach by overhanging trees, or when the mosquitoes have been quite beyond the powers of pennyroyal, is not yet sufficiently dim in memory. Considered as a class they seem to me about as pious as the exigencies and trials of their sport permit. If there has been any deterioration in this respect since the time of Walton—and it is greatly to be hoped that the average American fisherman is at least as well-conducted as Charles Cotton, Walton's friend and collaborator—the reason may be that the streams frequented by English anglers in the seventeenth century were not over-hung by alders and that English mosquitoes are not as a rule carnivorous. With regard to contemplation also the anglers of my acquaintance have fallen short of those that Walton knew, at any rate in outward demeanor. Some of them may have been disposed to find "books in the running brooks, sermons in stones," but they have all been decently reticent about reading those books and preaching those sermons to others. Not one of them, after losing a large fish or smashing a favorite rod-tip, has ever attempted in my presence to "justify the ways of God to men," but all have conveyed the impression that this task was beyond their powers. (I have already said that fishing is a little more like life than actual living is, and here I may add that fishermen are likely to seem rather more human, both for good and ill, than ordinary human beings engaged in ordinary activities.)

Concerning Father Izaak's opinion that anglers are remarkably industrious, gentle, and honest, however, I feel that something ought to be said, because this opinion is exactly counter to a widespread conviction in the minds of those who do not care for fishing that anglers are lazy, cruel, and sadly addicted to lies. These charges are probably very old; in our own time, fretfully and even bigotedly humanitarian and energetic as it is, they are made with disgusting frequency. It is high time they were answered. In attempting to answer them I shall not try to prove the truth of Walton's proud assertions and implications, nor shall

THY ROD AND THY CREEL

I attempt to sustain Thomas Tod Stoddart in his declaration that anglers are a superior race of men; it will be sufficient to show that they are as honest and humane as most people and quite energetic enough.

Lazy fishermen do of course exist, just as there are lazy bankers and clergymen and college professors and stevedores. Only yesterday I saw one of them: he was perched on a great blue boulder in the middle of a river when I went by at eight in the morning, fishing for bass with a float, and when I returned somewhat after sunset he was still perched on that boulder in what seemed the same attitude, perhaps with the same helgramite on his hook. If I had stopped to ask him about his luck he might have returned the classic answer, that to be sure he had caught no fish but that he had had "a glorious nibble." This was not so much fishing, however, as day-long dozing—and in a most uncomfortable position at that. I have seen old men on the piers stretching into Lake Michigan near Chicago who have scarcely stirred from dawn to dusk except to drag up now and then a wriggling perch or to impale a reluctant worm; and other ancient men I have seen—yes, and ancient women—on the piers reaching out into the Pacific who seemed to ask no more in the way of excitement than a run of yellowtail once or twice in a season. This was not fishing but basking. And then there are the Londoners who dangle hooks in the lower Thames, and the Parisians

THREAD OF THE RIVER

who sit on the banks of the Seine under umbrellas and go in seriously for *la pêche*—queer people, not one of whom have I ever surprised in the act of landing so much as a minnow. Again, there are the drowsy creatures who take a boat at noon-day and row out to the middle of a Wisconsin lake, drop anchor and hook there, and sit until sunset, "as idle as a painted ship upon a painted ocean." Probably it is from such common spectacles as these that the ignorant public had acquired its notion that angling is a lazy man's sport. Witnessing a five-hour battle with a tarpon or tuna, or actually holding the rod for a single minute of that conflict, would leave a different impression. Casting for salmon for a week or so without getting a single rise would convey to the dullest critic the notion that fishing is sometimes hard work. It is fair to test this matter in terms of fishing in what I take, perhaps somewhat arbitrarily, to be its highest form—trout-fishing in swift water. No one who will read the present book needs to be told that this is no sport for a lazy man. It tasks to the utmost every nerve and muscle and sinew, almost every sense, and nearly every faculty of the mind. Speaking as an amateur pedestrian and angler, I believe that the careful fishing of a mile of mountain stream requires as much energy as walking ten miles on a country road, and that any one who has fished three such miles has certainly earned a night's repose.

THY ROD AND THY CREEL

But no doubt the charge of laziness brought against the angler has often a deeper origin than mere honest ignorance. It is sometimes made by people who know well enough that true angling is a strenuous sport but who hate it as a waste of time and assert that it does no one any good. People who say this sort of thing—the "social servants" and professional uplifters and earnest busybodies with whom the streams of society are now so grievously over-stocked—enhance the charms of angling and other varieties of solitude by their mere existence. The shortest way to answer such persons—the shortest way, that is, other than preserving that complete silence which is most eloquent—would be to admit, or rather to re-assert with emphasis, that fishing does no good to any one unless it be to the angler himself, and that a man might fish every day of the open season throughout a long life without leaving the world thereby a whit better than he found it. And then one might continue, as though by way of after-thought, to say that such a man, during the fishing season at least, would be minding his own affairs, interfering with no one, condemning no one's way of having a good time.—But it is a sufficiently familiar fact that Americans have as yet no sound tradition or theory of leisure, and this is not the place to provide one. The sort of person who condemns angling because it "does no good" must have a whole book to himself, if he is to have his mouth properly stopped and is to be covered with the wholesome confusion he has long deserved. At present I can only recount to him a remark once made to me by a doctor of medicine: "Apples are a valuable article of diet because, so far as we can find out, they contain no food, have no medicinal properties, and, in general, do us no good." I like that "because," and indeed the whole statement is about the wisest utterance I have ever heard from a physician. By this time, no doubt, "science" has discovered that apples do us good, but I shall not try to find out because I am fond of apples and should like to go on eating them.

No angler worthy of the name particularly cares whether people think him lazy or not, but he is likely to be somewhat more sensitive to the equally common charge of dishonesty. Why this should be so it would take a long time to explain, because a good many wise men of the past have been rather pleased to hear others comment favorably upon their talents in deception. Nowadays, however, we seldom find a man who enjoys being called a liar, and no man enjoys the assumption that he must be a liar because he likes to go fishing. There is a *non sequitur* hidden away somewhere in the unspoken argument which is repugnant to all clear thinking.

Do I mean to deny, then, that the weight and length of captured fish, and still more frequently the length and weight of fish that "got away," are sometimes over-estimated in subsequent accounts? By no means. I know that they are. A friend of mine has recently told me of an experience he had once at a fishing camp in the Rangeley Lakes, where it was customary for each angler, when he came in for the night, to set down in a book the weight of his largest trout—depositing the same trout beside the book by way of evidence. On a certain day my friend and his father had taken a lake trout that drew their very accurate scales to three pounds ten ounces. Carrying this in to the counter and laying it beside the trout taken that day by the other men in camp, they found it by a good deal the largest of the lot. Somewhat surprised they were therefore, and then indignant, but finally amused and delighted, to discover that the weights set down in the book for those smaller fish were all considerably larger than that which they had just found their own trout to come to. The highest of these other weights happened to be eight pounds and a little over. Naturally, they glanced at the largest of the trout lying before them and made a simple arithmetical calculation: this trout is to ours as eight pounds is to—well, say eleven pounds. And so they set down eleven pounds as the weight of their fish and took the prize for that day.

There are some people who would consider that whole episode reprehensible and who would remember it as an example of the dishonesty of anglers. Of course it is in reality only another proof of the fact that anglers are men gifted in imagination, the highest faculty of the mind. Like the lover, the poet, and the madman, they are "of imagination all compact," and they have this trait in common with all other artists, that they strive in their representations to convey not so much the low and relatively unimportant truth of actuality as the higher truth of feeling. In describing a large trout or salmon they paint a portrait of him, which of course includes a free admixture of their own personalities and hopes and wishes, instead of merely snapping a camera.

We do well to remember, also, how memory and imagination work together in adding ounces and inches—nay, pounds and feet—to the fish of yesteryear. An infant troutling, just emerged from minnowhood, lying fair as drowned Ophelia in a fern-filled creel, is one thing to an ichthyologist or to a game-warden and quite another to the boy who has just had his first experience with rod and line. And when that sportsman thinks back, thirty years later, to his first trout and sees it in his mind's eye as about two feet long, shall we say that he is dishonest because of the slight discrepancy between his estimate and that which a prying scientist or custodian of the game laws would have made? His recollection tells him the truth of feeling, and in these matters that is at least an important aspect of what we naïvely call "the whole truth."

And at this point a word must be said concerning that ancient gibe, a stupid one even when it was first made, to the effect that if we believe anglers' tales it is "always the largest fish that gets away." How stupid this is even the ignorant ought to be able to see if they will consider that the chances a fish has of escape after he is hooked increase directly as the square, or perhaps even the cube, of his weight. This is to say that it is not merely three times as hard to take a three-pound trout as to take a trout of one pound but at least nine times as hard, to say nothing of the relative difficulty of inducing the rise. Usually, although not by any means always, it is the large trout that breaks one's tackle and smashes one's tip. Usually it is the large trout that "nimbly harnesses himself," as old Saunders puts it, "among the Weeds and the Roots of Trees." It appears, in fact, that until a trout reaches the weight of one pound he is a venturesome, audacious creature, trying to eat nearly everything that comes his way, disposed to look on the bright side of things and give the world the benefit of every doubt, but that after he has attained that majority he grows more and more suspicious and melancholy, sulking in the bottom of his pool and thinking up ways of making things hard for anglers. "Always the biggest fish that gets away"? Why, naturally.

THREAD OF THE RIVER

Here we have one reason for the tall tales to be heard in every well-regulated fishing camp. In the course of his experience every angler has hooked and lost a good many trout that he never saw clearly if at all. They are to him no more than extremely vivid memories of gigantic tugs followed by sickening slackline, or perhaps of darting gold deep in an amber pool —of gold that fled forever into the El Dorado of the fancy. The angler cannot help wondering what sort of finned giant it could have been that suddenly bent his rod double and then departed, carrying off a length of tackle as though it were so much cobweb. He cannot help picturing that mighty and mysterious fish, and his guess at its weight will vary from year to year— always upward. It is thus that legends grow, and myths—not in the mouths of liars but of poets. Every old fisherman keeps in his memory a whole aquarium of escaped fish that grow from decade to decade as though fed upon the "worm that never dies." I myself carry about with me a small tankful of such recollections, and I am not ashamed to say so. Mightiest of all is that of a trout I lifted once up the wall of a hundred-foot gorge in the Rocky Mountains—lifted, and dangled, and pulled up hand over hand—a rod is not for such work—until not more than ten feet of solid granite withheld him from my yearning eyes, and then dropped. "It vexes me to this day." It is one of the many things that go to convince me of the vanity of human wishes. I caught no glimpse of that trout, so that he is to me purely a muscular memory, yet he is still wonderfully vivid, and I can almost see him now as he went up that granite wall, glistering in the sunshine among the ferns, up, and up—and then so abruptly down. At the moment of our parting I should perhaps have estimated his weight at about two pounds, but now, after he has floundered and fattened all these years in the stream of my fancy—well, trout do not really grow so large as I remember him to have been.

The only charge brought against angling that has ever really troubled me is the charge of cruelty. I admit that I have given this one a good deal of thought, feeling that if it is true, as a good many persons have asserted with heat and rancor, that the angler gets his pleasure by giving pain, then my own pleasure in the sport must suddenly cease. Of course it is only in recent decades that we have been plagued by such problems. Until two hundred years ago most civilized persons really did take pleasure in witnessing pain, and if we are to include Spain and Mexico among civilized countries it appears that many do even now. In the earlier eighteenth century such questions would have been answered out of hand by referring to one of the many passages of the Bible in which fishing is mentioned without reprehension, and especially to the text in which we are told that God gave to man dominion over the fish of the sea. Somewhat later, the "argument from design" would have been applied inversely, to show that if the Creator had not intended fish to be caught by hooks he would not have provided them with horny mouths. (I have seen hunting defended by an obscure clergyman of the nineteenth century in this same way, by the argument that if God had not intended us to hunt he would not have "created" the setter and the bloodhound. Those were easier times to live in, when an educated man could make his brain work in that docile and convenient way.)

My own trouble began when I read Leigh Hunt's essay on Angling, the only essay of his in which I have found nothing to enjoy. With all the skill of his experienced pen and with the ardor of an advanced liberal who spent most of his days fighting with forlorn hopes for causes that seemed lost, Hunt drives home unforgettably his belief that the angler's pleasure—though it does not consist, like the Sadist's, in giving pain—is possible only where pain is given. "Let us imagine ourselves," he says, "a sort of human fish. Air is but a rarer fluid, and a supernatural being who should look down upon us from a higher atmosphere would have some reason to regard us as a sort of pedestrian carp. Now, fancy a Genius fishing for us. Fancy him baiting a great hook with pickled salmon, and twitching up old Izaak Walton from the banks of the river Lea, with the hook through his ear. How he would go up roaring and screaming, and thinking the devil had got him!"

It would take courage to say such things as that in England even today—except at a meeting of the Society for the Prevention of Cruelty to Animals, where every member says what he pleases, and especially about his fellow-members. A century ago and more, Hunt's words were those of a brave as well as a brilliant man, and I think we must respect the spirit of them if not the knowledge and experience they show. Leigh Hunt's experience and knowledge of fish and angling approached zero. Furthermore, although certainly courageous enough in all his human relationships, he was one of the "tender-minded" who are so sensitive to pain themselves as to be constantly imagining pain where it does not exist. He put himself, as it were, in the place of the fish—and this may seem a helpful and clarifying thing to do until one begins to recall some of the several respects in which Leigh Hunt—journalist, romantic poet, and whimsical essayist—differed profoundly from the most sensitive trout that swims. And even Izaak Walton, although Hunt irreverently traces a piscine resemblance in his features and calls him "a pike dressed in broadcloth instead of butter," was remarkably different in his feeding habits from any fish of prey. Suppose Walton had gone through just the experience

THREAD OF THE RIVER

that Hunt imagines for him—would he have been snapping at another bait of pickled salmon within half an hour after wriggling the hook of the Genius out of his ear? But that is precisely the sort of thing that trout are constantly doing.

This argument that because human beings would dislike to be pulled about with hooks in their gullets they ought not to treat fish so is seen in all its feeble sentimentality in a set of verses by Peter Pindar:

> *Oh, harmless tenant of the flood,*
> *I do not wish to spill thy blood;*
>   *For Nature unto thee*
> *Perchance has given a tender wife*
> *And children dear to charm thy life,*
>   *As she has done to me.*
>
> *Enjoy thy stream, oh harmless fish!*
> *And when an angler for his dish,*
>   *Through gluttony's vile sin,*
> *Attempts, a wretch, to pull thee out,*
> *God give thee strength, oh gentle trout,*
>   *To pull the rascal in!*

This is most affecting, but one is sorry to say that the sweet domestic scene it brings before us is remote from the facts. The father trout, instead of keeping his dear children about him to charm his life is strongly inclined to "make of his generation messes."

He believes that the children should support the parent, and his affection for his tender wife scarcely differs during most seasons of the year from that which he shows toward any other article of food. Indeed, the savage ferocity and rapacity of fishes must be seen to be believed, and *salvelinus fontinalis,* in spite of its lovely looks, is as ferocious, in proportion to its size, as the shark. An experiment conducted some decades ago in Boston proved that he can hold his own even with the mailed warrior called the black bass. Two dozen of each of the two species were placed together in a large tank and left to forage for themselves upon themselves. At the end of the time allotted it was found that the tank contained four trout and four black bass, all the rest having been telescoped into these eight fish, like the cook, the captain, the mate, the boatswain, the midshipmite, and sundry other members of the crew of the Nancy brig.

One fears that the destiny of almost all the young trout born into this harsh world—let us say, conservatively, of ninety-five in the hundred—is, simply, to be eaten alive. Many are eaten by minks, more by king-fishers, still more by herons, more still by bass and pickerel and pike, but most of all are eaten by trout. A single large cannibal trout—and all large trout are cannibals—will eat more trout in a month than an expert angler can take in a season. If we may indulge the casuistry, therefore, it may seem almost an act of mercy for the angler to withdraw that cannibal from the stream. The difficulty is, however, that in so doing he will only be giving the survivors time to attain cannibalistic prowess of their own.

I hope that all this will not sound utterly hard-hearted. Let me say that I have killed "for sport" in my life time just one warm-blooded creature—an English sparrow which I shot with a pebble from a sling when I was eight years old. Whenever, since then, it has been suggested that I might enjoy hunting I have seen the slowly thickening glaze of that sparrow's eye, and I have been quite sure that I should not enjoy it. The fox-hunting that I have seen as an innocent by-stander, though spectacular and exciting to witness, has been distasteful to me, and the stag-hunt as now practised in England is a horror. When I have heard the thirsting deer steal by my tent after midnight in the California mountains, my sympathy has been entirely with them rather than with the cut-throats who would be on the trails at dawn. Frankly, I do not understand how any one can shoot a bird or beast for pleasure, or for any reason other than the maintenance of human life. This I say not to
> *Compound for sins I have a mind to*
> *By damning those I'm not inclined to,*

but simply to make as clear as I can my belief that a man may be fond of fishing without being fond of slaughter for its own sake. Another way to show this would be to cite the names of a few well known fishermen. Will any champion of the trout against his own kind undertake to charge Lord Grey of Falloden or Charles Kingsley with cruelty? Does any one wish to say that John Burroughs or Mr. Bliss Perry has shown himself insensible to the pain of other creatures? The most skilful fishing companion I have ever had was a Quaker who served as a non-combatant in the Great War and who never raised a gun at any living thing; his sensibility to the pain and sorrow of the world approached the morbid degree; he spent the best years of his life in the world's best laboratories studying the nervous systems of the lower animals, including fish. If any man on earth has ever been equipped to do full justice to the trout from the trout's point of view, my friend was such a man; yet he fished with an enthusiasm that I have seldom seen equalled. He it was who helped me to recover from the effects of Leigh Hunt's essay.

The fact is that extremely few wild creatures of any sort die of what are called "natural causes," such as disease and old age. The rest are carried off by violence of numberless kinds. To our recently acquired sensibility this fact is a painful one, but our compassion should be expended nearer home. No animal dies as we do, with foreknowledge of death and with the consciousness of all that death brings to an end. We must adjust ourselves without loss of gentleness to the fact that nature has always been and must always be "red in tooth and claw," for otherwise we travel a road that leads to all manner of absurdities.

Probably the best object upon which to direct any sympathies that may be withdrawn from fish would be the human animal. It is still too early for us to forget that we have recently slain and mangled in the western civilized world—otherwise known as the Christian world—the bodies of several millions of young men. (The figures vary, but even if we accept the lowest estimate, eight million, that number of trout taken during four years in the several countries concerned would have been a very respectable catch.) I make the comparison because I have observed that not a few persons who denounce trout-fishing as cruel regard the killing of young men—of course I mean when it is done by wholesale methods—as a rather glorious occupation, entitling the survivors to high encomiums, political office and financial rewards. And indeed there is a difference between catching trout and killing youths, although it is not of a sort to justify the attitudes mentioned. The young man's family feels the loss of him more keenly, for one thing, than the trout's family can reasonably be supposed to feel the loss of one of their number. The young man has high hopes and memories, wishes and dreams, consciousness of self, awareness of pain, foreknowledge of death, love of life, and the trout has none of these. Again, it is to be remembered that trout can be raised from the eggs in hatcheries with very little trouble; young men are more expensive, and far harder to replace when their numbers have been depleted by a few exceptionally active open seasons.

There is nothing to be said against our modern sensibility. It has done no harm in the world, and it has done a vast deal of good; but now and then, here and there, a portion of its energy is deflected from worthy objects and lavished where it does not belong. While our lynching statistics remain what they are and so long as the nations continue to prepare for another haul of young men, the trout may be left to fend for themselves, as most of them know very well how to do.

Of course the really germane question, concerning which only a biologist can speak with anything like authority, is this: How much pain does a trout suffer in the course of a clean capture at the hands of an expert? The answer given me, by men whose knowledge and intelligence I trust, is that he suffers no pain whatever, as we understand pain. To find himself suddenly pulled up and down a pool instead of pulling other creatures up and down, as he has been accustomed to do, is no doubt a rude shock to his sense of the fitness of things—unless, indeed, he is one of the veterans who have often taken their morning exercise at the end of an angler's line. Probably he does not particularly dislike the experience of having a fly run away with him so long as it drags him downstream, but as soon as up-stream dragging begins he does begin to feel some discomfort, for during this process he is drowning. A trout brought to the net after a certain amount of play, including up-stream travel, is usually a trout half-drowned. Then follows—from the hand of an expert, let us remember—a sharp blow on the base of his brain which he feels not at all because it brings the end of feeling, and his brief trouble is over. Would that half of us, or any, could hope to die with so little pain, with so little anxiety to ourselves and others, with the same dash and headlong courage in the clutch of fate, leaving no more grief behind. As compared with being eaten alive, this is a luxurious euthanasia.

If trout suffer keen anguish while being "played," what do they suffer it with? Not with any such brain or nervous system as ours; not with any powers of anticipation or of memory or of realization that "this is I who is suffering." Take all these away, and what would pain amount to, even to us? No; the argument from trout to human beings which I have illustrated in passages from Peter Pindar and Leigh Hunt is no argument at all. It is mere rhetoric. An immense gulf separates us from the cold-blooded creatures. Assume that they suffer as we do, and the lives they live, the myriad terrible deaths they die will not bear think-

THY ROD AND THY CREEL

ing of. Agree with Leigh Hunt and his kind that we should never do to the lower creatures except as we would be done by, and not only will vegetarianism triumph at once but we shall soon have a Society for the Prevention of Cruelty to Vegetables, and before long there will go up the cry prophesied by Mr. G. K. Chesterton, "Why should salt suffer?"

Izaak Walton, as I have said, would soon have learned caution in snatching at baits of pickled salmon after he had once been taken on a hook and line dangling out of the firmament. Trout also learn caution, but less rapidly than we might expect them to do if their sufferings on a hook are really comparable with those that Walton would have had. I remember taking a three-pound trout in a Nova Scotia pond that had several small notches in its caudal fin. Counting these notches, my guide told me that this particular trout had been captured four times before. He then cut another notch and returned the fish to the water entirely uninjured—even improved somewhat, perhaps, by the wholesome exercise. I should like to know how many notches he has acquired by this time, supposing that he still swims in the upper waters of the Roseway River, and whether his appetite for Parmacheenee Belles is what it used to be. Fishermen who catch trout with rod and line for breeding purposes find that they lose hardly one in the hundred by injuries caused

THREAD OF THE RIVER

in capture, so that the mortality statistics range about even with those of the operation for appendicitis.

On the whole, therefore, it does not seem that fish particularly object to being hooked and dragged about, or if they do then they are blessed with short memories. I have heard Dr. Henry Van Dyke tell a story—amply vouched for by his avocation as a clergyman—about hooking a good trout three times running in one summer evening. It took first a red fly, perhaps an ibis, and ran away with it; then a blue fly was offered and similarly accepted. Finally a white miller brought him to net—and it was only when the angler saw his three flies—red, white, and blue—in the trout's mouth that he remembered that this quiet day in the mountains had been the glorious Fourth of July.

But now that I have done my best to refute the charges most commonly brought against anglers by ignorant and bigoted critics, I do not know that I have accomplished anything worthy of the effort. However cogent and unanswerable my arguments may have been, I shall not have convinced the slanderers, and neither shall I have told good anglers anything but what they already know. The most consoling thing to be said is this, that while one is working up a stream, at any rate, one forgets entirely the sort of people who make the sort of remarks I have mentioned—or if one thinks of them at all it is only for a moment and with some variation upon the helpful adage: "They say! What do they say? *Let* them say!"

The main point I have wished to convey, even at the risk of some tedium, is that a good angler is likely to be a good man. Farther than that I do not wish to go. My experience does not permit me such enthusiasm as that expressed by Stoddart, the mighty Scot: "Anglers are a more gifted and higher order of men than others, in spite of the sneers of pompous critics, or the trumpery dixit of a paradoxical poet. In their histories there are glimpses snatched out of heaven—immortal moments dropping from Eternity upon the forehead of Time." One sees that Stoddart was a poet, as he showed in a good many excellent angling songs, and that he is disposed to claim the privileges of the order; but even if he had not been that, a little harmless bombast in praise of his own craft should be allowed to so excellent a rod.

VI

ONE does not at first see why it is that anglers should care at all what is said of them as a class or should take the trouble to defend themselves. Their sport is solitary. It teaches them independence, it drives thought inward; yet they have always shown strong *esprit de corps* and many of them have gone a little out of their way to assert things in their own honor which persons really indifferent to public opinion would have left unsaid. Other classes of men do not do this. One never hears a dentist assert that dentists "are a more gifted and higher order of men than others, in spite of the sneers of pompous critics." What makes this difference?

I think we must conclude that a large part of the praise of anglers, as spoken and written by themselves, belongs to a greater and far more important controversy that has been going on ever since human beings began to think and express their thoughts. It is a minor aspect of the argument for solitude as against multitude, for the individual as against society, or, if one prefers, for contemplation as against action. One sees how this argument has gone in the western world during the last three centuries and more: multitude, society, and action have won at every turn,

THY ROD AND THY CREEL

so that the angler finds himself in a pitifully small minority. What wonder that he is sometimes a bit vociferous? Five centuries ago nearly every wise man would have been on his side, and in the East today he would find much good company, but as matters stand with him he is almost alone. He represents, moreover, a highly important principle, and whether he knows it or not he speaks for a good deal more than angling when he praises his own mystery. He stands for leisure, quiet, inner peace, in a world that has almost forgotten what these words once meant.—But Walton has said all this for me in Piscator's discourse to Venator during The First Day:

"I shall tell you that in ancient times a debate hath arisen, and it remains yet unsolved, whether the happiness of man in this world doth consist more in contemplation or in action? Concerning which, some have endeavored to maintain their opinion of the first; by saying that the nearer we mortals come to God by way of imitation, the more happy we are. And they say that God enjoys himself only by a contemplation of his own infiniteness, eternity, power, and goodness, and the like. And upon this ground, many cloisteral men of great learning and devotion prefer contemplation before action. And many of the fathers seem to approve this opinion, as may appear in their commentaries upon the words of our Savior to Martha.

THREAD OF THE RIVER

"And on the contrary, there want not men of equal authority and credit, that prefer action to be the more excellent; as namely, experiments in physick and the application of it, both for the ease and prolongation of man's life; by which each man is enabled to act and do good to others, either to serve his country, or do good to particular persons: and they say also, that action is doctrinal, and teaches both art and virtue, and is a maintainer of human society; and for these, and other like reasons, to be preferred before contemplation.

"Concerning which two opinions I shall forbear to add a third, by declaring my own; and rest myself contented in telling you that both these meet together and do most properly belong to the most honest, ingenuous, quiet, and harmless art of angling.

"And first I shall tell you what some have observed, and I have found it to be a real truth, that the very sitting by the river's side is not only the quietest and fittest place for contemplation, but will invite an angler to it: and this seems to be maintained by the learned Peter du Moulin who, in his discourse of the fulfilling of the Prophecies, observes that when God intended to reveal any future events or high notions to his prophets, he then carried them either to the deserts or the sea-shore, that having so separated them from amidst the press of people and business and the care of the world, he might settle their mind in a quiet repose, and there make them fit for revelation."

All this derives from the very ancient idea that a man is better for having as little as possible to do with the world, and from the idea of which I have already spoken that in the wilderness one converses with the Divine. In most of the classic literature upon angling it is assumed that the angler lives all the time in the country and devotes his leisure, at all seasons of the year, to his favorite sport. This means, at the least, that he is kept out of evil associations, is harmlessly employed, and it is the innocency of his pursuit that writers of the earlier periods make most of. "Indeed, my good scholar," Piscator remarks in a famous passage, "we may say of angling, as Dr. Boteler said of strawberries; 'Doubtless God could have made a better berry, but doubtless he never did'; and so (if I might be judge) God never did make a more calm quiet innocent recreation than Angling." This is modest and moderate. By the time of Thomas Tod Stoddart the Romantic Movement had caused a great up-stirring and renovation and misunderstanding of ancient notions about the relation of man to nature, among which none was more influential than the belief that one who lives alone in the wilds attains, in some vague unspecified way, a sort of wisdom and virtue never to be gained from human associations. We have recently recovered from this romantic extravagance—I do not mean to imply that our gain thereby has been unmixed—so that it is now possible and usual for anglers to think of themselves no more highly than they ought to think.

If I were trying to praise the expert angler in reasonable terms I think I should begin by speaking of the range and minuteness of his knowledge. He is in some sort a learned man, even though he may not be able to read. In this connection I should like to quote a paragraph or two from Gervase Markham's *Young Sportsman's Delight*, although I know that they set a high standard and are likely to be a bit discouraging to beginners. "A Skilfull Angler," says Markham, "ought to be a generall scholer, and seene in all the liberall sciences, as a grammarian, to know how either to write or discourse of his art in true and fitting termes, either without affectation or rudenes. He should have sweetness of speech to perswade and intice others to delight in an exercise so much laudable. Hee should have strength of arguments to defend and maintain his profession against envy or slander. Hee should have knowledge in the sunne, moone, and starres, that by their aspects he may guess the seasonablenesse, or unseasonablenesse, of the weather, the breeding of the stormes, and from what coasts the winds are ever deliviered. He should be a good knower of countries, and well used to high wayes, that by taking the readiest parth to every lake, brooke, and river, his journies may be more certaine and lesse

THY ROD AND THY CREEL

wearisome. Hee should have knowledge of proportions of all sorts, whether circular, square, or diametricale, that when hee shall be questioned of his diurnal progresses, he may give a geographicall description of the angles and channels of rivers, how they fall from their heads, and what compasses they fetch in their several windings. Hee must also have the perfect art of numbering, that in the sounding of lakes and rivers hee may know how many foot or inches each severally contayneth, and, by adding, subtracting, or multiplying the same, hee may yield the reason of every river's swift or slow current. Hee should not be unskillfull in musick, that whensoever either melancholy, heavinesse of his thought, or the perturbation of his own fancies stirreth up sadnesse in him, he may remove the same with some godly hymne or antheme. He must then be full of humble thoughts, not disdaining, when occasion commands, to kneele, lye down, or wet his feet or fingers, as oft as there is any advantage given thereby unto the gaining the end of his labor. Then hee must be strong and valiant, neither to be amazed with stormes nor affrighted with thunder, but to hold them according to their natural causes and the pleasure of the Highest. Neither must he like the foxe which preyeth upon lambs imploy all his labour against the smallest frie, but, like the lyon, that seazeth elephants, thinke the greatest fish which swimmeth a reward little enough for the pains which he endureth. Then must he be prudent, that, apprehending the reasons why the fish will not bite, and all other casuall impediments which hinder his sport, and knowing the remedies for the same, he may direct his labours to be without troublesomeness."

Although this may seem what is vulgarly termed "a large order," it is at once apparent that Markham's passage is more remarkable for what it leaves out than for the qualifications it mentions. Indeed it seems unlikely that the author of it was a practical fisherman, considering that he says nothing about the knowledge of flies, of tackle, of bait, of the habits of fish, of water, of striking or playing or netting.—I speak under correction, but I doubt whether there is any other sport in the world that demands so much hard-won knowledge of the expert as angling does, and whether there is any other form of play that comes so near to learning.

It may be, however, that the qualifications mentioned by Gervase Markham were sufficient for the demands of his time, which was the time of Shakespeare. They would be quite inadequate for the consistent taking of twentieth century trout, educated as these have been to demand of us very much more subtle tactics than Markham seems aware of. A large trout of our day living in a hard-worked stream is to the most erudite trout of the early seventeenth century as Ulysses to Ajax, as Houdini to an alderman. Our fishing has to be finer, and is so, because the fish are more exacting. Even in Walton's time, what naïve and bungling methods on the angler's part were cheerfully accepted by the prey, as though they took the will for the deed and saw that all was well intended! Trout and dace and pike and carp came to Walton's hook with amazing docility, as though he were Adam and were calling them severally up to him by name; but they must have done this, so far as a modern reader can discover, chiefly out of good nature. Walton tells his pupil in the course of the lesson on trout that when he has hooked a very large fish he throws his rod after it into the water and then runs after it along the bank! This is one of the proofs he advances that "fishing is an art."

It is an art that has made rapid progress since Walton's time. To keep pace with the progressive enlightenment of fish we have found new materials for our rods and brought them down to feather weights, we have tapered our lines and leaders, perfected our reels, studied stream entomology, and greatly increased the number of artificial flies—of which Walton knew almost nothing at first hand. We have developed the theory of up-stream fishing and finally established it, after a long controversy; we have studied the problems of the trout's vision; finally, we have perfected the technique of the dry-fly and have taken to using it even for salmon. In short, we have learned to fish with a skill of which Walton and Cotton and Barker never dreamed; and yet it is evident that the English anglers of today do not catch more trout than their predecessors did, but fewer.

No angler tells today—at any rate without grievous straining of the truth—of any such personal exploit as that handed down for our admiration by Thomas Barker, the angling cook. At six o'clock of an evening he was told by his master, Lord Montague, to prepare several large dishes of trout for a great banquet to be held in the house on the morrow. Barker wasted no time in telling his Lordship that there was not a single trout in the house. He went immediately to the door "to see how the wanes of the air were like to prove," and finding the weather indications satisfactory he told his fellow-servants that he doubted not, God willing, to be provided with sufficient trout in good time. At sundown he was at the water equipped with certain lob worms, perhaps with salmon roe which he was apparently one of the first to use, and with three flies, white, black, and red—"the white flye for darkness, the red in medio, and the black flye for lightnese." With this outfit he fished from sunset to dawn, and so successfully that by noon of that day he had ready to serve something over a dozen dishes of trout—trouts in broth, four dishes of calvored trouts, marionated trouts, trout pies hot and cold, and

THY ROD AND THY CREEL

trouts broiled and fried and stewed and roasted!— Something has happened to English trout since that great draft of fishes was taken by one rod on a single night, and something has happened to anglers and angling in consequence. It is now a better sport, fit not only for cooks but for gentlemen.

VII

THE most obvious improvement has been made in the implements of the sport. In Dame Juliana's *Treatyse of Fysshynge wyth an Angle* we learn that the rod of the fifteenth century was of domestic manufacture and was composed of two main pieces, a six-foot "staffe" of hazel or rowan and a "croppe" of the same length. This croppe was also in two parts, the lower of hazel and the upper of juniper, crab, or blackthorn. All the pith was burned out of the staff or butt, and when one was not fishing the crop was telescoped into it so that it looked like a long walking-stick of the sort often carried by pedestrians in that time of savage dogs, and with this, says the *Treatyse*, "Ye may walk, and there is no man shall wit whereabout ye go"—a manifest advantage. Although the Dame assures us that this rod will be right light and full nimble to fish with, it does not compare favorably in those respects with the hexagonal split-bamboo. The butt of it had to be "as thick as your arm" and fitted with ferrules of iron or brass, and all of the crop was made of solid and heavy wood, so that it must have been in reality about as light and nimble as a twelve-foot sapling. Emphatically, this was a "two-handed engine," and a day's sport with it must have been about as exhausting as any ordinary day at hard labor. By Walton's time good rods were obtainable in the shops of London—eighteen to twenty feet in length and composed of a dozen pieces of wood lashed together. (It is a strange bit of piscatorial history that although the reel, or winch, and the jointed rod with ferrules were both known to the author of the *Treatyse,* these devices were not used by the classic anglers of two hundred years later.) Imported woods began to take the place of native materials at the end of the eighteenth century—greenheart, lancewood, bamboo, and—most common if not most important of all—American hickory. The last stage of perfection in rod-making was probably initiated by the gun-maker Samuel Phillipe of Easton, Pennsylvania, whose bamboo rods in six sections began to come on the market some ninety years ago. Doubtless man can make better rods than these fairy wands weighing one or two ounces that have descended from Dame Juliana's hollow tree, but doubtless he has not yet done so.

The lines of the fifteenth century, like most lines of the three centuries following it, were made of white horse hair, variously colored. The *Treatyse* advises that several hairs be twisted together, but this made coarse fishing which the trout could not be expected to put up with permanently. Charles Cotton thought two strands sufficient. Thomas Barker, the cook, asserted that the single hair is far more effective than the twist of two or three and that with proper handling it will hold the largest trout that swims— one of those ample trout mentioned by Walton as large enough to "fill six reasonable bellies."

This fishing with a single hair must have been decidedly sportsmanlike, and one is glad to know that it lasted well on into the nineteenth century, long after silk lines and well-drawn leaders were available to all. Some angler with a liking for the old-fashioned who cares more for the delicacy of his technique than he does for the taking of fish would do well to revive it—as I dare say a good number are even now attempting to do. For the encouragement of such enthusiasts I quote this record of an angler who appeared just a hundred years ago at an angler's inn, The Swan, at Thames Ditton, near Hampton Court:

"One evening last summer there alighted from the coach a gentleman, apparently of the middle age of life, who, first seeing his small portmanteau, fishing-basket, and rods safely deposited with the landlord, whom he heartily greeted, walked into the room and, shaking hands with one or two of his acquaintances, drew a chair to the window, which he threw up higher than it was before; and, after surveying with a cheerful countenance the opposite green park, the clear river with its sedgy islands, and the little flotilla of punts, whose tenants were busily engaged on their gliding floats, he seemed as delighted as a bird that has regained his liberty: then, taking from his pocket a paper, he showed its contents to me, who happened to be seated opposite, and asked if I was a connoisseur in 'single hair'; for, if I was, I should find it the best that could be produced for love or money. I replied that I seldom fished with any but gut-lines; yet it appeared, as far as I could judge, to be very fine. 'Fine!' said he, 'it would do for the filament of a spider's-web; and yet I expect tomorrow to kill with it a fish of a pound weight. I recollect,' continued he, 'when I was but a tyro in the art of angling, once fishing with an old gentleman whose passion for single-hair was so great that, when the season of the year did not permit him to pursue his favorite diversion, he spent the greatest part of his time in travelling about from one end of the kingdom to the other, seeking the best specimens of this invaluable article. On his visits to the horse-dealers, instead of scrutinizing the horses in the customary way, by examining their legs, inquiring into their points and qualities, or trying their paces, to the unspeakable surprise of the venders, he invariably walked up to the nether extremities of the animals and seized hold of their tails, by which means he was enabled to select a capital assortment of hairs for his ensuing occupation.' " (Have I not said that trout-fishing is English? Who but an

THREAD OF THE RIVER

Englishman could have spent his time on such a hobby—or could have described it with such delight?)

Even in the time of Samuel Pepys there were innovators abroad, for we read in his Diary under date March 18, 1667: "This day Mr. Caesar told me a pretty experiment of his angling with a minikin, a gutt-string varnished over, which keeps it from swelling, and is beyond any hair for strength and smallness. The secret I like mightily." Robert Venables, a better angler than Pepys is known to have been, though not a better than that amazingly versatile man might have been if he had given time to it, was in that very year using lute and viol strings for his casting lines; and this too would have been mightily liked by Pepys the amateur musician.

At first thought one is likely to suppose that the greatest advance in the art of angling during the last four hundred years must have been made in the invention and manufacture of artificial flies. These are now so numerous, and they are so beautiful even to the eye of the tyro, that the mere sight of a large flybook well stocked is enough to breed respect for the sport in one who has been ignorantly contemptuous, and to convince him that a great many years of experience must have gone to make it what it is. Such a deduction would be entirely sound. It would also be properly based, for it is really an astonishing fact that eleven of the twelve flies described in the *Treatyse of*

THY ROD AND THY CREEL

Fysshynge wyth an Angle are still in common—I might almost say universal—use both in England and America. And yet it seems probable that a great deal of the ingenuity expended in developing the hundreds of feathered lures now displayed in shop windows has been misspent, for most of them are better calculated to attract purchasers than trout, salmon, and bass. Local peculiarities in the entomological tastes of trout are of course to be allowed for—such, for example, as the keen enthusiasm they display for Parmacheenee Belles in Maine and the complete indifference they show toward them in Connecticut—and here is a legitimate excuse for the existence of many flies; but aside from this, and having reference to the broad catholic tastes of trout in all times and places, the "jury" of twelves flies listed by Dame Juliana, and reproduced more or less slavishly by a score of writers down to and including Izaak Walton, ought to be sufficient. A good fisherman seldom needs more flies, if they be well selected, than he can conveniently stick in the brim of his hat. When I say "well selected" I am thinking that his assortment should certainly include several brown hackles, one or two black gnats, and at least one bivisible. It may be no more than a social prejudice, but the fact is that when I see a man open a fat fly-book liberally bestuck with miniature rainbows I suspect him of being not an honest angler at all but of belonging to one of the more objectionable varieties of millionaires.

And yet there is a charm and beauty in artificial flies—most of all for those who make them with their own hands, no doubt, but a good deal for those who merely gaze at them and paw them over as they lie in their little white boxes at the shop. I like to look at them in a detached and purely spectatorial way, as I do at a collection of pictures that is not for sale. Once or twice I have thought of buying a considerable number of them and arranging them in patterns on the walls of my cabin, but this would be more expensive than almost any other kind of mural decoration. A good deal of this kind of decoration is done, out of doors to be sure, inadvertently and with no eye to the matching of colors. One may see it along the banks of the Neversink, and I know a popular little stream in Devonshire over which the artificial flies hang fluttering from the twigs like a host of tiny banners displayed in preparation for some gala event. One would think that Oberon and Titania were expected.

There is also a great quantity of lore concerning artificial flies—enough to engage the researches of a life time and to furnish forth a book that would attract a good many intelligent readers outside the ranks of fishermen. Most educated persons probably know already that they fall roughly into three categories: the flies that imitate actual species, those that

THY ROD AND THY CREEL

imitate genera, and fancy flies intended to look merely like insects. Most important of these are the fancy flies, of which Richard Franck remarks: "Among the variety of your Fly-adventureres, remember the Hackle, or the Fly substitute, form'd without wings, and drest up with the Feather of a Capon, Pheasant, Partrig, Moccaw, Phlimingo, Paraketa, or the like, and the Body nothing differing from the Fly, save only in ruffness and indigency of Wings." Even in this passage one gets a hint of the strange and far-fetched materials often brought together from the ends of the earth to cover the barb of a single hook. John Gay did not exaggerate the facts in his pleasing passage upon fly-tying:

> *To furnish the small animal, provide*
> *All the gay hues that wait on female pride;*
> *Let nature guide thee—sometimes golden wire*
> *The shining bellies of the fly require;*
> *The peacock's plumes thy tackle must not fail,*
> *Nor the dear purchase of the sable's tail.*
> *Each gaudy bird some slender tribute brings*
> *And lends the glowing insect proper wings.*
> *Silks of all colors must their aid impart,*
> *And every fur promotes the fisher's art.*

In his directions for tying the Grannom, Bowlker calls for peacock's herl, grizzled cock's hackle, mottled

THREAD OF THE RIVER

pheasant's feather, and the black fur from the face of a hare. He made the Blue Dun of cock's hackle, duck or starling feathers, fox fur, and yellow mohair. Charles Cotton made his Stonefly of the feathers of the grey mallard, brown and yellow camlet, bear's hair, and two or three hairs from a black cat's beard. The ingredients of some of the standard flies of today are almost identical with those employed to make the same flies five hundred years ago, and probably much earlier still. An attempt to find out who first made the Mayfly and the Red Spinner and the Grannom would lead the student on a merry chase into the Middle Ages and possibly into the ancient world.

Such a piece of research would graze now and then upon the macabre, as we discover in reading James Chetham's *Angler's Vade Mecum*. Under the rubric "Oyntments to alure fish to the baite" this seventeenth century expert directs us to "Take the Bones or Scull of a Dead-man, at the opening of a Grave, and beat the same into pouder, and put of this pouder in the Moss wherein you keep your worms." And the ointment in which he had even greater confidence was thus compounded: "Of Man's fat, Cat's fat, Heron's Fat, and the best Assafœtida, of each two Drams; Mummy, finely poudered, two Drams."—In reading such prescriptions one begins to comprehend the old-fashioned trade of Body-Snatching somewhat better. The same note is struck in a versified handbill put

THY ROD AND THY CREEL

forth as an advertisement some eighty years ago by an English tackle-maker:

> *When the old clock in yon gray tower*
> *Proclaims the deep, still midnight hour,*
> *And ominous birds are on the wing,*
> *I rise from the realms of the bony King.*
> *My bonny elm coffin I shoulder and take*
> *To fish in the blood-red phantom lake,*
> *Where many a brace of spectral trout*
> *Forever frisk, dart, and frolic about.*
> *Then the hyæna's ravening voice*
> *Gladdens and makes my heart rejoice.*
> *The glow-worm and the death's-head moth*
> *Are killing baits on the crimson froth.*
> *For work-bench I've the sculptured tomb,*
> *Where tackle I form by the silent moon;*
> *Of churchyard yew my rods I make;*
> *Worms from the putrid corpse I take;*
> *Lines I plait from the golden hair*
> *Pluck'd from the head of a damsel fair;*
> *Floats of the mournful cypress tree*
> *I carve while night-winds whistle free;*
> *My plummets are molded of coffin-lead;*
> *For paste I seize the parish bread;*
> *The screech-owl's or the raven's wing*
> *For making flies are just the thing.* . . .

THREAD OF THE RIVER

A human skull is my live-bait can;
My ground-bait, the crumbling bones of a man.

Artificial flies are second in attractiveness only to beautiful rods among the items of the angler's equipment, although he should strive to regard them not primarily from the æsthetic point of view but—as far as he can manage it—with the eyes of a hungry trout looking up at them from the brook's bottom and seeing them chiefly as little spots of light where the surface is indented. Such an effort of imagination will help him to avoid putting too much of his faith in colors, and so help him to catch fish. But a careful choice of leaders will help still more. Without the very tenuous and translucent leaders of our day we should be unable to take any good trout whatever in some of the best streams in the world. Modern reels have made it unnecessary—as well as highly inadvisable—for us to throw our rods into the stream and run after them, as Walton did. We are no longer obliged to make our hooks out of steel needles, as anglers did in the fifteenth century—although we should probably get stronger and sharper hooks by this process than can now be bought at the shops.

VIII

SO much for the implements, the tools and the toys, of angling; and I doubt whether those of any other sport, unless it be archery, can be brought into comparison with them for intrinsic charm. But beauty is the very stuff and essence of this sport. The trout-fisherman not only has beauty about him and in his hand; he pursues it as his quarry. Many fish more gaudily colored than the speckled brook trout of America—that is to say, the char—may be seen in any large aquarium, and some that are almost as perfectly shaped as he, but when this speckled brook trout is glistening and pulsating with the nuptial glow he is probably the loveliest thing that swims in sea or lake or stream. He varies from one valley to another, from stream to stream, even from pool to pool, but wherever one finds him in good condition and in the prime of his age he is beautiful. But why should we confine him to supremacy among fish alone? No beast of the land or bird of the air surpasses in loveliness

The trout, by Nature mark'd with many a crimson spot,
As though she curious were in him above the rest,
And of fresh-water fish did note him for the best.

THREAD OF THE RIVER

After taking several trout in succession one may grow inured to their beauty so as to ignore and forget it; but then one may draw up, after a brief and pusillanimous struggle, some dismal dace or perhaps the heart-sickening sucker, and then the trout's beauty is felt anew in its absence. Or else, much more rarely, one may bring to net a trout that stands forth as a paragon even among trout as Helen of Troy did among women, and thus again his eyes will be opened. One such I can see before me as I write, although it is nearly fifteen years ago that I caught him accidentally while trolling for coarse fish in a lake in Maine. His head and shoulders and oddly aquiline nose were deepest purple, or seemed so until one saw the deeper purple of his eyes, and this color, with which he was saturated and suffused, ebbed softly away down his sides. All his fins, as I remember them, were purple also, but along his belly were great streaks and splashes of vivid crimson. (Just what he was I do not know. Perhaps a "blue-back," or perhaps an Alpine trout strayed down from Canada—and then again, perhaps unique, like the Phœnix.) Altogether, he looked like an unusually gorgeous little sunrise as he lay there on the gunwale of my boat, making no strenuous effort to escape but merely opening and closing his mouth in well-bred protest. I looked at him; I enlarged my former conception of the splendors that the world contains; then I unhooked him very gently and put

THY ROD AND THY CREEL

him back into the water. It would have been an indignity to dump him into my basket with a mess of scoundrelly bass and pickerel; and as for preparing him for supper, I should almost as soon have cooked a baby angel.

Of course there is the best possible reason for the aristocratic appearance and manners of the Salmon family: they are vastly older, as a family, than most other fresh-water fish. They were here before the great glacier. For a good many hundreds of years they must have lived in the vast dark rivers of the under-earth, there acquiring their taste for cold and perfectly pure water, perhaps also their marvellous strength and ability to "thrive against the current." If we wonder that trout should be able to feed at midnight we may find the explanation in this long training of theirs in perfect darkness. Whether they were albinos when they came to the surface again or whether they were pitch black, I do not know, but certainly they have made good use of their time in the sun and scarcely any other fish adapt themselves so quickly to the general hues of their environment. Trout are the chameleons of the water.

Even those of the *salmonidæ* that do not go down to the sea are wide travellers, if we think not of the individual but of the species. They travel by cloud and water-spout, in the stomachs of migrating birds and in the pelican's bill. Add to these means of transport the recent assistance of man, which has brought the German trout to America and the rainbow of the Rockies to the eastern States, and it is no wonder that the trout is now fairly well distributed over the globe. (I was about to write "the *habitable* globe," but I considered in time that no part of the earth can properly be called habitable if it is entirely troutless.)

Everywhere he goes he does us good. Ranging through his beneficences from low to high, one may say that he eats numberless insects that we should be glad to get rid of, that he draws into our State Treasuries every year large and increasing sums of license money that we are glad to have; that he provides a motive for forest preservation that goes home to the business and bosoms of many men who "could not be bothered" with that problem for any other reason, but who can at least understand that with no forests we shall have no trout; that he has fed our pioneers, lured our adventurers over mountain passes and across the continent; that he gives to the tame and tired slaves of the machine some taste of the adventure in the wilderness that was their fathers' daily fare; that he draws many thousands every year into associations good for body and mind and soul; that he provides us with recollections that shine with ever deepening luster as our lives wear on into time.

IX

THE memory of an old angler is rich with innumerable spoils and trophies of the past; it is vivid, detailed, exact. Something in the nature of the sport makes our angling memories more enduring than others, and even the man who has difficulty in recalling his own address or the maiden-name of his wife can see the flashing arrow of dull gold made by a trout that he took—or lost—thirty years ago, as clearly as though it were now arching his rod. Though he may have no manual skill in other things, he remembers every knot that has been explained to him by the stream-side or over the evening fire, and the ability to tie them sleeps in his fingers from season to season. Every observation he has ever made in fishing, however minute, has contributed something to his present skill, so that he seems to know by instinct, at the first glance over a pool, where the trout will lie, how they are to be approached, and in what order. Every mistake he has ever made now warns him, and every success guides hand and foot and eye as he works his way along strange water. He has acquired what may be called a bodily wisdom, which is really a host of dormant memories and the deductions, often un-

THREAD OF THE RIVER

conscious, that he has made from them.—How does he know, for example, just when and how hard to strike a rising trout? The interval of time to be allowed varies widely according to speed of current, the size and habits of the trout concerned, and the nature of his lure; much depends also upon the particular rod he is using, the length of line, even the time of day and of season. No theoretical statement taking all these factors into account can possibly be made to guide him, nor can he consciously think what to do in the fraction of a second allowed. All one can say about this rather mysterious matter of striking is that the good angler draws upon his hoard of memories, assorts them instantly, chooses those that are pertinent to the present situation, which is always exceedingly complex, and then—does the right thing. Not always, to be sure, but with surprising frequency. A man might read books about fishing until overcome by blindness and never learn to strike properly. He must try and fail and try again, remembering why he failed, supposing that he can find out. A good angler may forget freely and profusely about every other matter; he remembers everything about angling.

But of course his memories are by no means confined to the difficult and never-perfected technique of taking fish. All the environment of his sport, as I have tried to show, shares in the strange vividness of his recollection. One source of the charm in Walton's book is the pellucid clearness of the vignettes he draws, and these little pictures of field and tavern and stream are clear because they were first painted clearly on the walls of his memory, so that all he had to do in writing was to gaze at them steadily and then transfer them as best he could into words. There is something delightfully specific in Charles Cotton's writing about the sport also, which almost brings to the reader's ear the chuckle and murmur of his River Dove, just as in John Dennys and William Brown of Tavistock we constantly hear brook water bubble and roll and lave and rumble zigzaggedly down. They had some secret, those fresh-voiced enthusiasts of the seventeenth century, which enabled them to take their readers along on their fishing excursions. William Browne was an amazingly fluviatile poet, and I never read him without smelling the indescribable sweet damp musty odor of river water, without seeing the six-foot spikes of Canterbury bells that tower in June on either side of the Lynn and Tavy. And then there is William Gilbert, a little known man who published his *Angler's Delight* in Walton's time and who had the same secret of seductive particularity. While discussing the method of fishing in Hackney Marshes he advises the reader to "go to Mother Gilbert's at the Flower de Luce, at Clapton, near Hackney, and whilst you are drinking a pot of ale, bid the maid make you two or three pennyworth of ground-bait and some

THREAD OF THE RIVER

paste (which they do very neatly and well)." That is how an angler remembers.

Or consider this passage of reminiscence from Walton himself, probably the most famous in all angling literature: "Look! under that broad beech-tree I sat down, when I was last this way a-fishing; and the birds in the adjoining grove seemed to have a friendly contention with an echo, whose dead voice seemed to live in a hollow tree near to the brow of that primrose-hill. There I sat viewing the silver streams glide silently towards their centre, the tempestuous sea; yet sometimes opposed by rugged roots and pebble-stones, which broke their waves, and turned them into foam; and sometimes I beguiled time by viewing the harmless lambs; some leaping securely in the cool shade, whilst others sported themselves in the cheerful sun; and saw others craving comfort from the swollen udders of their bleating dams. As I sat thus, these and other sights had so fully possest my soul with content, that I thought, as the poet has happily exprest it:

> *I was for that time lifted above earth,*
> *And possest joys not promised in my birth.*"

It was a happy man who drew that picture, and he was happy in the recollection, wonderfully fresh and clear, of a day spent with rod and line. All good anglers have memories such as this, and, whether they know it or not, such scenes as this are a part of their mental sustenance when icicles hang by the wall. They feed on these as the hibernating bear is kept alive by the berries that grew on the hills of summer. Such recollections are more precious by far than anything to be taken with a rod and brought home in a creel. It is for these most of all that we go fishing—and these, happily, no conspiracy of the elements and no bungling or ignorance of our own can keep from us. Angling is in many ways one of the most uncertain of sports, yet the angler may always be perfectly sure of his reward.

This is a mystery incomprehensible to those who look from outside. Some years ago I engaged a Connecticut inn-keeper to carry me in his car at dawn to the banks of a certain distant stream and to call for me in the evening. It was raining hard when we set forth, and only with difficulty could I make him understand that I proposed to fish in spite of the weather, and even if we were in for another Noah's flood. When he put me down at the stream and saw me set forth into the down-pour his fat sides were shaking with laughter. Every hour of that April day it rained harder than it did the hour preceding, and I was as wet after ten minutes in the alder thicket as I should have been if I had stepped hat-high into the first pool. Yet all that day I fished in perfect content, catching,

THREAD OF THE RIVER

if I remember correctly, three seven-inch trout as the tangible portion of my prize. When I climbed at last into my landlord's car—lamed by distance and leaping from rock to rock and sundry falls, streaming as though I had brought a small tributary of the brook along with me—and exhibited the day's catch, the delight of that humorsome person passed all bounds, and he laughed so hard all the way home that he could scarcely hold the wheel. He is laughing still at that day's fishing, and telling about it with justifiable adornments and addenda to most of his patrons; when he sees me coming down the road his fat sides begin to shake and heave before I arrive within hailing distance.—On the whole, I count that lonely day in the rain on which I took three tiny trout as one of the best days I have ever spent. This is a mystery, as I have said, to those who look on. It is worth seeing from the inside.

And now to all good anglers who have read to the end of this book—the patience elsewhere learned standing them here in good stead—I wish as good a day as that, and a larger catch, when next they go a-fishing. May they cast their flies into beauty and draw them back over the waters of peace.

THE END